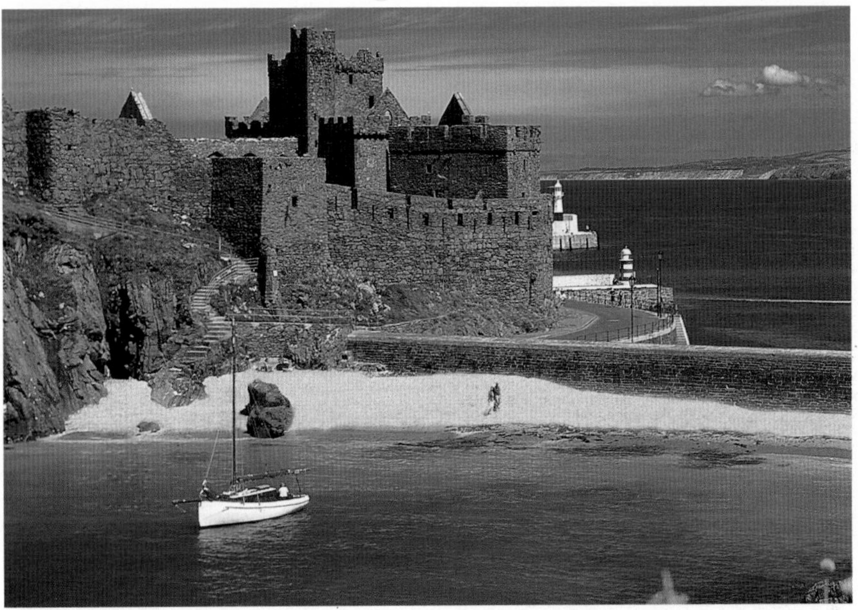

Above: Peel Castle
Front cover: Ramsey harbour
Back cover: Ballabeg Station

Written by: Andrew Douglas & Stan Basnett

Revised: Miles Cowsill, Rob Penn and Alf Alderson

Photography: Lily Publications, Michael Thompson, and Dept. of Tourism & Leisure

First published by Lily Publications 1994

Second (revised) edition 1996
Third edition published 1998
This (4th) edition published 2000

 Published by Lily Publications (IOM) Ltd, PO Box 9, Narberth, Pembrokeshire, Wales SA68 0YT. Tel: +44 (0) 1834 891461/2, Fax: +44 (0) 1834 891463.
ISBN 1 899602 85 2.

Contents

Maps

Welcome

In the Isle of Man we take our tourism very seriously and it was with the greatest of pleasure that I accepted the invitation to write the foreword to this, the *Premier Guide to the Isle of Man.* Within the pages of this very attractive and highly recommended book you will find all the ingredients to help you make your visit enjoyable and informative.

Our traditions and heritage are many and varied and in some instances unique to our small Island kingdom. We have, for instance, the oldest continuous parliament in the world, over 1,000 year old and using the same system of government given to us by our Viking forefathers. We still have our steam trains, which celebrated their 125th year of operation in 1998, electric tramcars over 100 years old, and to this collection can be added horse drawn trams that traverse the entire length of the elegant Douglas promenade. Definitely not to be missed is the matchless international award winning "Story of Mann". Join it at the Manx Museum, or at the new "House of Manannan" in Peel, or at any one of the many sites dotted about the Island, and experience how life used to be in our nation.

Niarbyl Bay

Contained within our borders is a collection of scenery without equal. A land of gently sloping sandy beaches, rocky coves, sheer cliffs, valleys, thickly wooded glens, rolling hills, mountains and a castle or two thrown in for good measure. A patchwork quilt of beautiful countryside just waiting to be explored. Rich in culture, there are events and attractions galore, sufficient to cater for the needs and tastes of even the most discerning of holidaymakers.

The Isle of Man which in our own Manx Gaelic we refer to as Ellan Vannin extends a warm welcome and as a member of Tynwald, the Island's Parliament, I am pleased to extend to you an invitation to come on over and see us. I know you will not be disappointed.

David Cretney.

Hon David Cretney MHK
Minister
Isle of Man Department of Tourism and Leisure

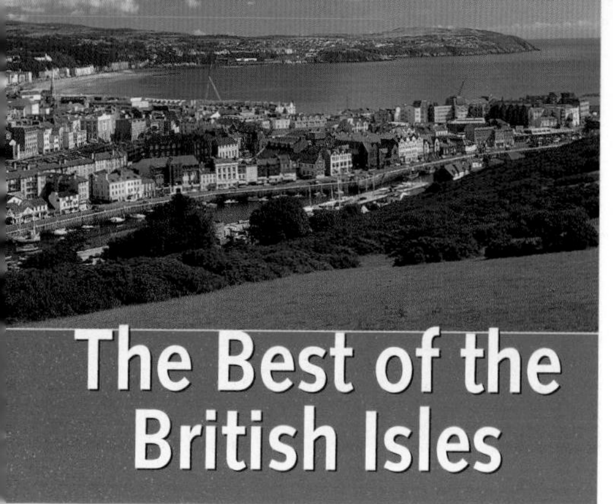

The Best of the British Isles

Geographically the Isle of Man lies midway between the coasts of England, Ireland, Scotland and Wales. The Island measures at its extremities 33miles (52kms) by 13 miles (22kms) and has a land mass area of some 227square miles (572 sq. kms). It has a wide variety of scenery covering virtually every type found elsewhere in the British Isles, ranging from stretches of open moorland to thickly wooded glens and palm fringed ponds.

Encompassed within over 100 miles (160kms) of coastline there is a central range of mountains and hills lying in a north easterly/south westerly direction with well defined valleys leading down to rocky cliffs and sheltered bays. This contrasts with the flat northern plain's lazy rivers and streams meandering down to long sandy beaches.

The Isle of Man has a temperate climate, lacking in extremes due to its location and the warming influence of the Gulf Stream which flows around the shoreline. Prevailing winds blow from the south west, giving varying degrees of shelter and exposure island-wide due to the rugged nature of the topography. The warmer days and increasing hours of daylight of March and April are proving increasingly attractive to visitors, whilst in summer the months of May and June are usually the driest, and May, June and July are the sunniest. July and August are the warmest and more often than not, September and October enjoy fine weather.

In recent years there has been a growth in the resident population to the present level of some 73,000. This gives a density of 321 people per square mile (127 per sq.km) and with about 40% of the Island being uninhabited there is always plenty of room to move around. The major centre of population is Douglas, the capital, with approximately 22,500 residents – a further 28,000 people live in seven other main towns and villages. The Isle of Man has the oldest continuous parliament in the world, its own currency, stamps, telecommunications, language, castles, legends and customs - despite its apparently close links to the rest of the British Isles.

So, although you can see every other country in the British Isles from our shores, it would be a mistake to think the Isle of Man is simply another part of Britain - it is very much a separate and unique corner of the world.

The mighty Laxey Wheel

FAILT ERRIU

Neayr's traa erskyn towse, ta Mannin er jebbal da goaldee shilley jeh dy chooilley red va mie ayns ny shenn laghyn, kianlt seose marish roie-ennaghtyn jeh'n traa ry-heet. Ga dy vel ee beg, v'eh rieau cheet lhee dy hoilshaghey magh yn aalid as eunys eck, skeayley magh yn chaghteraght shen dy roshtyn gagh ard jeh'n chruinney.

Ta Ellan Vannin sy vean, eddyr Sostyn, Nerin, Nalbin as Bretin – 'ny hellanyn sniessey'. Ta lhiurid smoo yn Ellan 33 meeiley (52 km) as ta'n lheead smoo 13 meeiley (22 km), as she 227 meeiley kerrinagh (572 km kerr.) yn eaghtyr-thallooin jee. Shimmey reayrt-cheerey ta ry-akin ayns Mannin, goaill stiagh bunnys gagh sorch dy reayrt ta ry-akin ayns Ellanyn Sheear ny hOarpey, goll veih reeastaneyn mooarey gys glionteenyn lesh ymmodee biljyn gys puill chemmit lesh biljyn-palm. Cheu-sthie jeh 100 meeiley (160 km) as ny smoo jeh slyst-marrey, ta dreeym meanagh dy 'leityn as crink ta goll veih'n Chiar-hwoaie gys yn Cheear-ass lesh coanyn coon ta goll sheese dys eayninyn creggagh as baieaghyn fasteeagh. S'mooar yn anchaslys eddyr shen as awinyn as strooanyn litcheragh y thalloo rea twoaie ta goll dy moal dys ny traieyn geinnee liauyrey ayns shen.

Ta emshyr Vannin kenjal dy liooar kyndagh rish y voayl t'ee ayn, as ee goaill soylley jeh chiow y 'Trooan Gulf, ta goll mygeayrt-y-mooee. Ta'n thalloo sleitagh cur fastee ny lhiggey y raad da'n gheay neear-ass, y gheay chliaghtagh. Ta ny turryssee cheet dy choontey ny smoo jeh'n emshyr ayns Mee Vayrnt as Averil, ta sharaghey lurg y geurey. Sy tourey, ta Mee Boaldyn as Mean-souree cliaghtey ve ny meeghyn smoo chirrym, as ta'n emshyr smoo grianagh ayns Mee Boaldyn, Mean-souree as Jerrey-souree. She Jerrey-souree as Luanistyn ny meeghyn s'choe, as, son y chooid smoo, ta emshyr vraew ry-gheddyn ayns Mean-fouyir as Jerrey-fouyir.

Er y gherrid, ta earroo cummaltee Vannin er nirree gys red goll rish 70,000. Ta shen dy ghra, cha nel agh 321 persoonyn ayns gagh meeiley kerrinagh (127 ayns gagh km kerr.). Cha nel sleih cummal ayns 40% jeh'n Ellan, as myr shen ta kinjagh rheamys dy liooar dy gholl mygeayrt ayn. Ta'n chooid smoo jeh ny cummaltee ayns Doolish, yn ard-valley, lesh red goll rish 22,000 cummaltee. Cheu-mooie jeh shen, ta 28,000 dy 'leih cummal ayns shiaght baljyn elley.

Shimmey yindys t'ayns y cheer shoh, ta glass, taitnyssagh as feer hroaragh! Yn ard-whaiyl shinney sy teihll va chaglym gyn scuirr, as ny reddyn elley shoh s'lesh yn Ellan neesht: yn argid eck hene, ny cowraghyn-postagh, chellinsh, y chengey, cashtallyn, skeealyn as cliaghtaghyn. T'ad ooilley cheet ry-cheilley lesh ram reddyn elley dy yannoo 'Yn Ellan Shiant' ass Mannin. Tar harrish as fow magh dhyt hene.

BIENVENUE

Depuis la nuit des temps, visiter l'île de Man c'est découvrir un peu ce qu'il y a eu de bon dans le passé tout en ayant un avant-goût de l'avenir. En dépit de sa petite taille, l'île a su témoigner de sa beauté et de ses merveilles aux quatre coins du monde.

Géographiquement, l'île de Man se trouve à mi-chemin entre les côtes anglaises, irlandaises, écossaises et galloises: les îles environnantes. L'île mesure à ses extrémités 52km sur 22km pour une superficie de 572km_. Elle présente une grande variété de paysages couvrant pratiquement tout ceux que l'on trouve dans les îles Britanniques: de grandes étendues de landes sauvages, des gorges couvertes de forêts denses, des étangs bordés de palmiers. Ceinturée de plus de 160km de côtes, la chaîne centrale de montagnes et de collines, orientée du nord-est au sud-ouest, possède de magnifiques vallées encaissées aboutissant à des falaises rocheuses et des baies abritées. Quel contraste saisissant avec la plaine uniforme du nord où les méandres des rivières et des cours d'eau aboutissent à de grandes plages sablonneuses!

L'île de Man jouit d'un bon climat, sans températures extrêmes, grâce à sa position et à l'influence du Gulf Stream qui réchauffe son littoral. Les vents soufflent principalement du sud-ouest et la nature escarpée du relief donne à cette île de grands contrastes avec des endroits exposés et d'autres abrités. Dès la fin de l'hiver, les visiteurs apprécient déjà l'amélioration progressive du temps au mois de mars et d'avril. En été, les mois de mai et de juin sont généralement les plus secs et mai, juin, juillet les plus ensoleillés. Juillet et août sont les plus doux et très souvent il fait encore beau en septembre et octobre.

Ces dernières années, la population a augmenté pour atteindre actuellement environ 70 000 habitants. Ceci représente une densité de 127 habitants au km et comme 40% de l'île est inhabitée, il y a encore beaucoup de place. Une grande partie de la population est concentrée dans la capitale, Douglas, qui compte environ 22 000 habitants, les sept autres villes et villages principaux regroupent 28 000 personnes.

Ce pays verdoyant, plein de charme et extrêmement fertile réserve bien des surprises! L'île a le plus ancien parlement du monde en exercice sans interruption, sa propre monnaie, timbres, télécommunications, langue, châteaux, légendes et coutumes. Il y aurait bien plus à dire sur l'île de Man, le joyau des îles Britanniques, alors il vaut mieux y aller soi-même pour découvrir ses merveilles.

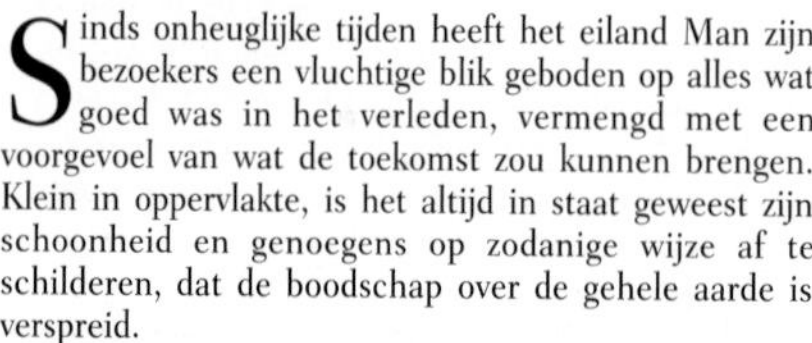

WELKOM

Sinds onheuglijke tijden heeft het eiland Man zijn bezoekers een vluchtige blik geboden op alles wat goed was in het verleden, vermengd met een voorgevoel van wat de toekomst zou kunnen brengen. Klein in oppervlakte, is het altijd in staat geweest zijn schoonheid en genoegens op zodanige wijze af te schilderen, dat de boodschap over de gehele aarde is verspreid.

Geografisch gezien ligt het eiland Man in het midden tussen de kusten van Engeland, Ierland, Schotland en Wales – "de aangrenzende eilanden". Het eiland meet tussen de uiteinden 33 bij 13 mijl (52 bij 22 km.) en heeft een oppervlakte van ongeveer 227 vierkante mijl (572 vierkante km.). Het biedt een grote verscheidenheid aan natuurschoon met vrijwel elk type dat elders op de Britse Eilanden te vinden is, variërend van uitgestrekte heides en dik beboste bergdalen tot met palmen omzoomde plassen. Omringd door meer dan 100 mijl (160 km.) kustlijn ligt een centraal bergketen in een noordoost/zuidwestelijke richting met duidelijk begrensde valleien die naar steile rotsen en beschutte baaien aflopen. Dit vormt een kontrast met de trage rivieren en stromen die zich van de noordelijke vlakte naar de lange zandstranden aldaar omlaag slingeren.

Het eiland Man heeft een gelijkmatig klimaat zonder uitersten tengevolge van zijn positie binnen de verwarmende invloed van de Golfstroom die langs de kust stroomt. De heersende wind is zuidwestelijk en tengevolge van de ruwe topografie wordt men hier afwisselend tegen beschut en aan bloot gesteld. Het beter wordende weer tegen het einde van de winter in maart en april blijkt steeds aantrekkelijker te worden voor bezoekers. In de zomer zijn de maanden mei en juni gewoonlijk het droogst, terwijl mei, juni en juli het zonnigst zijn. Juli en augustus zijn het warmst en meestal is het in september en oktober mooi weer.

In de laatste jaren was er een groei in de vaste bevolking naar het huidige niveau van ongeveer 70.000. Dit geeft een bevolkings- dichtheid van net 321 personen per vierkante mijl (127 per vierkante km.) en daar ongeveer 40% van het eiland onbewoond is, is er altijd genoeg bewegingsruimte. Het belangrijkste bevolkingscentrum is Douglas, de hoofdstad, met circa 22.000 inwoners, terwijl er nog 28.000 wonen in zeven andere grotere steden en dorpen.

In dit groene, aangename en zeer vruchtbare land liggen veel verassingen! Het eiland heeft het oudste onafgebroken parlement ter wereld, zijn eigen muntstelsel, postzegels, telecommunicaties, taal, kastelen, legendes en douane, en dit alles samen met nog veel meer maken het eiland Man... "Engeland's best bewaarde eiland". Kom zelf maar kijken.

WILKOMMEN

Seit Urzeiten bot die Insel Man ihren Besuchern einen flüchtigen Eindruck von allem, was in der Vergangenheit gut war – verbunden mit Erwartungen dafür, was die Zukunft bringen würde. Obgleich sie klein ist, hat sie es stets verstanden, ihre Schönheit und Köstlichkeiten in das rechte Licht zu rücken und sich in einer Weise mitzuteilen, daß sie jeden Winkel der Welt erreichte.

Geographisch liegt die Insel Man in der Mitte zwischen der englischen, irischen, schottischen und walisischen Küste – "den Nachbarinseln". Die Insel mißt an den äußersten Punkten 52 km mal 22 km und hat eine Landmasse von etwa 572 km². Sie bietet die verschiedensten Landschaftsbilder, wie sie an anderen Stellen auf den britischen Inseln zu finden sind, von offenen Hochmoorflächen, dicht bewaldeten Tälern bis zu mit Palmen umringten Teichen. Von über 160 km Küste umgeben, verläuft in nordöstlicher/südwestlicher Richtung in der Inselmitte ein Gebirgszug mit gut ausgebildeten Tälern, die in felsigen Klippen und geschützten Buchen enden. Dies steht im Kontrast zu den träge fließenden Bächen und Flüssen der flachen nördlichen Ebenen, die sich zu langen, sandigen Stränden schlängeln.

Auf der Insel Man herrscht ein ausgeglichenes Klima ohne Extreme, bedingt durch ihre Lage und den Einfluß des warmen Golfstromes, der ihre Küste umspielt. Der Wind weht meist von Südwesten. Dabei ist die ganze Insel durch ihre zerklüftete Topographie unterschiedlich geschützt oder dem Wind ausgesetzt. Nach Ende des Winters erweist sich das bessere Wetter im März und April für Besucher immer attraktiver. Im Sommer sind die Monate Mai und Juni gewöhnlich am trockensten, während Mai, Juni und Juli am sonnigsten sind. Juli und August sind am wärmsten, und in den meisten Fällen herrscht im September und Oktober schönes Wetter.

In den letzten Jahren nahm die Bevölkerung auf den derzeitigen Stand von etwa 70.000 zu. Damit entsteht eine Bevölkerungsdichte von ganzen 127 Einwohnern pro Quadratkilometer, und da etwa 40% der Insel unbewohnt sind, bietet sie immer genug Bewegungsfreiheit. Douglas, die Hauptstadt, hat die meisten Einwohner, etwa 22.000. Weitere 28.000 wohnen in sieben anderen größeren Städten und Dörfern.

Das grüne, angenehme und sehr fruchtbare Land bietet viele Überraschungen! Die Insel kann sich des ältesten fortgesetzten Parlaments der Welt rühmen, einer eigenen Währung, eigenen Sprache, Briefmarken, eines eigenen Fernmeldewesens, Schlössern, Legenden und Gebräuchen, und durch alles zusammen und vieles andere wird die Insel Man zur "beliebten Insel Großbritanniens". Besuchen Sie uns. Überzeugen Sie sich selbst.

The West coast of the Island

Getting to and around the Island

Getting to and from the Island has never been easier. Updated information on all air and sea services can be obtained from the various carriers direct or your local travel agent. If you can, try and book early as there are certain periods in the year when the Island is extremely busy and advanced booking is the only sure way of ensuring you get tickets for the journey of your choice.

Ferries

The Isle of Man Steam Packet Company, founded in 1830, operates a modern fleet of vessels and during the summer sails from four UK and Irish ports with the main all-year- round UK ports being Heysham and Liverpool. Each of these ports is served by good roads and often by rail/bus connections. The Steam Packet have full booking facilities with British Rail and National Express, and if you are travelling in a group of ten or more by rail/sea or just by sea, ask for details of their special group fares. Magic Holidays – the company's package holiday division – can also arrange your entire trip.

The Isle of Man Steam Packet Company also runs conventional and fast ferry services to the Island from Belfast and Dublin.

Manx Airlines

Air

Manx Airlines operate direct services from thirteen UK and Irish airports. Additionally there are a number of other airports throughout the British Isles and Europe which offer onward connections to the Island through British Airways Express with whom Manx have a strong connection.

Established in November 1982, Manx Airlines' modern fleet of aircraft has a distinctive livery emphasised by the national motif on the tail, and the words Skianyn Vannin, Wings of Man, near the front of the aircraft.

Manx Airlines involve package holiday operators in their plans and elsewhere in the guide are adverts from local package holiday operators. Group travel is available with Manx, although if you're coming over to enjoy the Island's excellent golf courses it's advisable to let the airline know so they can make appropriate arrangements for your clubs.

Additional air services are offered by Jersey European (0289 0457 200) and Comed Aviation (01253 402661).

Getting Around

Nowhere on the Island is geographically more than six and a half miles from the sea and the many roads and tracks criss-crossing the countryside soon bring you back to the coast.

There are good maps of the Isle of Man available and if you are a keen walker it's worth getting hold of the Isle of Man Public Rights of Way Map, which is published by

ISLE OF MAN

GO AT SPEED... GO AT LEISURE... GO IN STYLE!

By sea

Let the Steam Packet Company take you and your car to the beautiful Isle of Man in style. You can choose between the speed and exhilaration of our SuperSeaCat and SeaCat services, or the more leisurely pace of our conventional ferry 'Ben-my-Chree'. With first class onboard facilities, plus an extensive choice of year round sailings, there really is no better way to travel to this diamond in the sea!

SAILINGS

WINTER:
- Daily sailings from Heysham
- Friday, Saturday & Sunday sailings from Liverpool

SUMMER:
- Daily sailings from Heysham
- Daily SuperSeaCat or SeaCat sailings from Liverpool
- SeaCat sailings from Belfast and Dublin

For further information please call:

08705 523 523

SAILINGS FROM • HEYS HAM • LIVERPOOL • BELFAST • DUBLIN

Manx Electric Railway

Laxey Station

the Isle of Man Department of Local Government and Environment. The Ordnance Survey 1:50,000 Landranger map of the Island (sheet 97) is also well worth obtaining.

Horse Trams

Running the length of the Douglas Promenades, in front of the brightly painted hotels and guest houses, the horse trams are part of the town's Victorian heritage. Dating from 1876, they offer a leisurely trot between the Jubilee Clock to the Strathallan Terminus at Summerland, with numerous tram stops en route. The open air trams are known as "toast racks" - look at the first one you see and you'll understand why! The horses that pull the trams are specially trained for the work and the track is designed so that a man can actually pull, with ease, a fully laden tram along the full length of the route. The working conditions are good with short days - a two hour shift per day in the season and all winter off to enjoy the grazing - and that's just for the horses!

Douglas Corporation operates a pension

Horse Tram at Douglas

LET US DO THE DRIVING

Discover the Isle of Man with Isle of Man Transport. The Victorian Manx Electric Railway, Snaefell Mountain Railway and Steam Railway offer a unique way to enjoy the Island in a relaxed and leisurely fashion.

The Isle of Man also has a well integrated bus network making just about every part of the Island accessible.

So, from the top of Snaefell to Calf Sound, let Isle of Man Transport chauffeur you around our Island.

Special Freedom Tickets offer a variety of ways to enjoy the Island at your leisure by a combination of the steam railway, electric trams, buses and horse trams.

For more information please write to:

Isle of Man Transport
Transport Headquarters
Banks Circus
Douglas IM1 5PT

We've got just the ticket for you!

TRAIN & BUS ENQUIRIES
01624 662525

scheme for the horses and when the time comes to retire, a permanent home awaits them at the Isle of Man Home of Rest for Old Horses. You can visit the home on Richmond Hill, it's on the bus route to Castletown with a stop right outside and there is ample parking for cars by the stables. There are also facilities for the disabled.

Electric Trams

Strathallan Terminus at the north end of the bay houses the rolling stock and provides workshop facilities for the Manx Electric Railway. In 1993 the MER celebrated its centenary. The company uses the original rolling stock from the 1890s, and you may find yourself on board one of two of the oldest working tramcars in the world. They travel to Ramsey along a twisting and turning 17.5 mile route via the important railhead in the village of Laxey. There you will find the only mixed gauge railway junction in the British Isles from where you can switch to the Snaefell Mountain Railway, the only electrically operated mountain railway in the British Isles, and 100 years old in 1995 .

Mountain Railway

Change systems at Laxey for the four mile climb to the summit of the Island's highest point. The slow and gradual ascent up the side of Laxey Glen provides bird's eye views of the famous Laxey Wheel, restored and acting as a reminder that not so many decades ago Laxey was a centre for lead and zinc mining. After crossing the TT Course, the trams pause for a short while at the Bungalow Station before tackling the final stretch to the summit of Snaefell - in Manx Sniaul and Snoefjall from the Scandinavian meaning Snow Mountain. A short walk from the Summit Cafe brings you to the mountain's peak and superb views of the Island, England, Scotland, Wales and Ireland.

From Laxey, many tourists retrace their journey to Douglas past the pretty little stations of Fairy Cottage, Ballabeg, Baldrine, Groudle Glen and Onchan. Others head north via the stations of Cornaa, Ballajora and Dreemskerry to Ramsey. To commemorate the MER's centenary a new visitor centre was opened at the northern terminus, dedicated to the history of the railway. Ramsey played its part in the building of the Mountain Railway, for it was from there that in 1895 the ten year old steam engine "Caledonia" was sent by sea to Laxey. After careening the vessel in Laxey harbour the engine was moved on baulks and rollers through the village to the station to assist in the construction of the new railway. Steaming up and down the mountain daily without the benefit of fell brakes this, the heaviest engine in Manx railway history, did the job on the hand and steam brakes alone.

Groudle Glen

Steam Trains

The Isle of Man Steam Railway is one of the Island's unique institutions. From Douglas Station rolling stock that is almost 130 years old carries you through magnificent countryside to Port Erin in the far south of the Island, along 16 miles of well maintained track. It passes Ballasalla, historical Castletown and Port St Mary before reaching Port Erin. There is usually time to have a look around the railhead and

Getting to the Island

Steaming through the Manx countryside

Exploring the Island by car

the Railway Museum is certainly worth a visit. There is also a café, and the station's waiting rooms are full of railway memorabilia.

The Douglas - Port Erin line is all that remains of a network of steam railways which also took the traveller from the capital to Peel and Ramsey via the Island's central valley. The northern line branched off at St John's. From St John's, a railway line was laid up the glen to link Foxdale lead mines with the main line system.

In 1996 the Groudle Glen railway celebrated its centenary. This 2-ft gauge line climbs up out of the lower reaches of the glen and winds its way along the hillside through trees, gorse, bracken and heather to the clifftop terminus. The views are splendid and all the credit can be put down to the willing volunteers and supporters who worked hard to restore this marvellous little railway to its former glory. Normally only operating a regular service in the summer months there are 'specials' at other times of the year -check with the TIC's for details.

Buses

Isle of Man Transport also provides an Island-wide bus service as part of an integrated bus and rail public transport network. Bus times are usually carefully co-ordinated where possible with the trains and trams.

Coaches

Privately owned coaches also operate on the Island. Tours Isle of Man, offer morning, afternoon and evening mystery tours or full day round-the-Island tours as well as providing transfer services. The coaches depart from Douglas Promenade throughout the main tourist season.

Car Rental

There are a number of companies offering a full range of hire vehicles, from small economy vehicles to minibuses. Amongst these are Mylchreests, Athol Car Hire, Hertz Car Hire, Ocean Ford and Empire Garage. See advertisements on pages 59, 73,108 and 111.

Isle of Man Transport

The Great Sporting Island

If you can bear to sit and read instead of dashing out into the wild blue yonder here's a brief run-down of how to get your outdoor kicks on the Isle of Man.

(Please note that the Isle of Man Department of Tourism produces a number of leaflets to many of the activities described below – please call in at a Tourist Information Centre (TIC) for more details, or call 01624 686801).

Walking

Don't look here for details on walking! Check out the chapter specifically dedicated to one of Britain's most popular outdoor activities ('Walking on Mann'). There you'll find all you need to know about the excellent walking to be found all over the Isle of Man see pages 125-155.

Sailing

The Isle of Man has great sailing for everyone from novices (on the relatively calm waters of Ramsey and Douglas bays) to experienced sailors, who will enjoy the challenge of the Island's rugged north and south coasts.

Cruising, racing and dinghy sailing are all popular, and the main event each year is the Round the Island Yacht Race, although there are smaller events throughout the year.

The Isle of Man is a popular stopping-off point for sailors crossing the Irish Sea, and with the popularity of sailing amongst the locals there are six sailing clubs on the Island and a number of excellent and picturesque harbours, including Douglas, Ramsey, Port Erin, Peel, Laxey, Port St. Mary and Castletown.

The main harbours are as follows:

Douglas – good shelter except in NE winds, and very heavy seas in NE gales. Harbour Master – 01624 686627.

Peel – good shelter except in strong NW to NE winds when entry should not be attempted. Harbour office – 01624 842338

Port St. Mary – very good shelter except on E or SE winds. Inner harbour dries out. Port Manager 01624 833206 (also for Port Erin and Castletown).

Ramsey – very good shelter except in strong NE/SE winds. Harbour dries out. Port manager 01624 812245.

Laxey – sheltered except in strong NE/SE winds. Harbour dries out. Port manager 01624 861663.

Kayaking/Canoeing

A sea kayak is an excellent way of exploring the Island's beautiful and fascinating coastline, allowing you to get into otherwise inaccessible coves and bays, and to get up close to wildlife such as grey seals, dolphins and basking sharks.

For inexperienced or novice kayakers lessons are available from outdoor centres on the Island which will have you out on the water, exploring, on your first day. For more details call The Venture Centre at Maughold for more details (01624 814240) or the Manx Canoe Club on 01624 816551.

Windsurfing

Being an Island, and being subjected to the – let's say 'breezy' - conditions that are virtually an everyday feature of life in these latitudes means that as long as the wind is actually blowing, the chances are that somewhere on the Island you'll be able to get in a good day's sailing.

Derbyhaven in the south is a popular venue – for more details of this and other

Fishing at Port Cornaa

spots contact Manx Marine on 01624 674842.

Surfers may also find waves if they're prepared to search. Although we have no definitive details of breaks on the Isle of Man, a look at a map and the fact that the Island is ideally placed to pick up any swell moving up or down the Irish Sea makes it highly likely that, under the right conditions, rideable waves will be found by anyone prepared to make the effort. Call the Aquatec for details 01624 833037

Jetskiing

Like them or loathe them, jet skis are obviously here to stay, and if you do want to give one a go the calm waters off Douglas and Gansey are the place to head for.

Fishing

The Isle of Man has a wide range of options for fishermen, ranging from sandy beaches to rocky headlands and quiet riverbanks to upland reservoirs. River fishing may take you into the beautiful national glens of the Island.

River fishing is until the end of September, reservoir fishing until the end of October, and salmon and sea trout are mainly fished in late summer and autumn.

Where to fish...

The sea angling is excellent due to the varied coastline – from sheer cliff faces in the south to long, flat surf beaches in the north. You can also fish off breakwaters and promenades, such as at Douglas Harbour.

There are seven reservoirs where you can fish – West Baldwin, Clypse, Kerrowdhoo, Ballure, Sulby, Cringle, and Eairy. Angling is allowed between 06.00 or sunrise (whichever is the later) until 30 minutes after sunset or 22.30, whichever is the earlier.

The main rivers for fishing are the Dhoo, Glass, Neb, Silverburn, Santon and Sulby, and there are many smaller streams. You may catch salmon, sea trout, brown trout, and

Sailing off the coast of the Isle of Man

rainbow trout. The rivers and streams are regularly stocked with brown trout, but please note that there is a daily bag limit of six fish, of which no more than two may be salmon or sea trout.

The Island has two major angling events each year – Ramsey Angling Festival (July-August) – call 01624 812279 for details and the Mannin Angling Club Festival in Port St. Mary in August (01624 832623). This is a boat fishing festival for charter boats and smaller boats.

For a complete list of fishing locations and angling clubs and information on freshwater angling licences please call the Tourist Information Call Centre on 01624 686801.

Sub Aqua

Diving is a very popular activity on the Isle of Man, which has several diving clubs and a dive school. There's plenty of marine life to see beneath the waves, and some good wreck sites, although you should check on access before you head out to these – many are protected by the wreck laws and some are owned by local people or sub-aqua clubs.

The Calf of Man area in particular is worth an underwater visit, as the marine life here is particularly diverse.

For more information on diving on the Isle of Man call Port Erin Marine Biologist' Sub Aqua Club (01624 832027) or the Isle of Man Sub Aqua Club (01624 629886). Diving courses are available from the Southern Diving Lodge in Port St. Mary (01624 832943).

Cycling & Mountain Biking

The Isle of Man is ideal for exploring by bicycle, whether you want to stay on paved roads or head off road. With such a wide range of terrain from broad flat plains to mountains and coast there's something here to suit everyone from family groups to committed cyclists and mountain bikers.

Wherever you ride you'll be assured of great views of coast and countryside – and if you get up high enough you may also get to see Scotland, England, Wales and Ireland from the saddle – it's worth the effort!

The Tourist Information Call Centre (01624 686801) has a very useful guide for road cyclists featuring six routes from six to 27 miles in length taking in pretty much every corner of the Island. Maps of each route, plus route descriptions and details on cafes, pubs and bike shops make this a great introduction to cycling on the Island.

For off-road adventure, you will have to buy an OS map and find your way into the hills. It is not difficult to pick out a route as there is an extensive network of byways and farm tracks that wind across the hills. There are also a number of plantations, managed by the Forestry Dept., where you can ride. A couple of classic downhill runs start from near the top of Snaefell. One goes north, leaving the A18 at mountain Box, ending up in Ramsey, via Sky Hill where the Norseman Godred Crovan is reputed to have defeated the Manx in battle in 1075. The other route starts on the B10 and heads south to Baldwin, from where you can follow the road all the way down to Douglas. An excellent circular ride, involving a solid climb, leaves Ballaugh on the Ravensdale road, passes through the plantation, round Slieau Dhoo and then drops dramatically back down to Ballaugh.

Combining a bit of on road and off road riding, you can cross the Island in each direction, finding challenging riding and fantastic views. For more information on routes and news about competitions, contact the Manx Mountain Club (tel: Graham Hughes 01624 861448).

Pony Trekking

The wide variety of landscapes on the

Wet Zone

On course for great Golf

Island provide for some great pony trekking for all abilities. Beginner's can discover the country and coastline on quiet back lanes, whilst more experienced riders will enjoy the open moorlands and their expansive views across to the British mainland and Ireland.

For more details call the Tourist Information Call Centre on 01624 686801.

Golf

The Isle of Man has seven 18-hole golf courses and one nine-hole course, all of them set in magnificent countryside with spectacular views across coast and country. Queues are rarely a problem, and the small size of the Island make it easy to play all the courses in a week's visit if you're really keen!

Amongst the Island's courses are Castletown (01624 825435) with a beautiful links course which was used for the 1979 PGA Cup matches against the USA. It was laid out by golfing legend Mackenzie Ross in the late 20s and early 30s and provides some of the purest links golf anywhere in the British Isles; King Edward Bay (01624 672709) which has magnificent views across Douglas and the bay; and nine-hole Port St. Mary (07624 497387) which has one of the finest views on the Island from the sixth tee.

The Tourist Information Centre can supply you with a free pocket guide to golfing on the Island – call 01624 686766 for details.

National Sports Centre

And finally, if the weather isn't too great, how about enjoying your watersports indoors? The £10 million watersports complex at the National Sports Centre in Douglas has enough to keep you occupied all day. A 25 metre competition pool, a separate leisure pool with bubble tub, flow pool, jets and geysers, water cannon, mushroom sprays and a toddler's slide mean the entire family can have fun here. Even if it's not raining the centre is worth a visit at some point with it's great cafe! Call 01624 688588 for prices and opening times.

Cycling

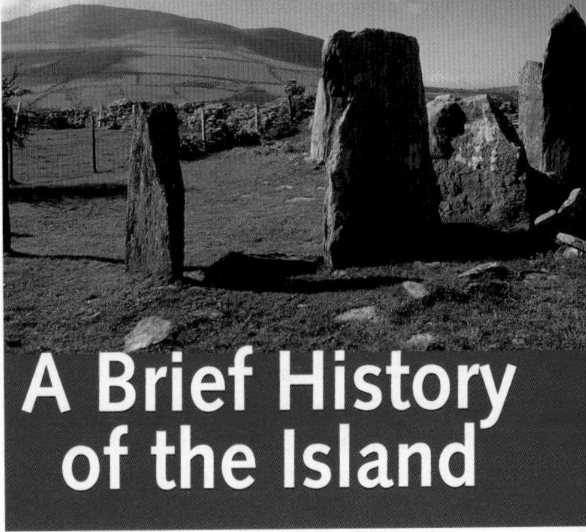

A Brief History of the Island

The history of the Isle of Man is a thrilling one, though it is so encrusted in the wealth of traditional lore and popular superstition that it is sometimes difficult to determine the fact from the myth. As Dr Johnson said: "All history so far as it is not supplied by contemporary evidence is romance." Nowhere is that more true than in the Isle of Man.

Early History

The Manx are a markedly Celtic race, though this is less obvious today. Despite the imposition of Scandinavian government absorbed from the Vikings, the people are Celtic by race and in outlook. It is likely, from the evidence, that the earliest inhabitants of the Island were a branch of the original Celtic people of the British Isles. The original Manx language (it has not changed and is now becoming more spoken again on the Island) is of the type of Gaelic spoken by the Highland Gaels and the Irish, and different from that spoken by the Bretons and the Welsh. The Celts inhabited Central and Western Europe in pre-Roman times and in all likelihood derived, by assimilation, from the Neolithic people in the British Isles.

Standing Stone, Maughold

Not much survives from this period save for a few old names. In Manx-Gaelic, the word for 'homestead' was 'balla' and there remain nearly 200 'balla' place-names today. Of the original Manx place-names, 70% are Celtic. Many Manx surnames date from the Celtic period also, though they have been altered. Many begin with a hard C, K or Q – Corlett, Kelly and Quayle – which are all shortened versions of the Mac prefix. So Corlett is MacCorleod, son of the fierce one.

Excavations have revealed that the Celts were a prosperous and peaceful people, closely interwoven with the Irish. They lived in communities, with an idiosyncratic land tenure system which was largely unchanged by the feudal system. During the period the Celts changed from Pagan to Christian and the existing monuments show this well. They left behind 'monuments' in the form of Ogham stones, and there are four fine examples in the Isle of Man that date from the 4th Century.

The Romans certainly knew of the Isle of Man, but they never came as settlers and their influence, though profound on mainland Britain, was negligible here.

The Coming of the Norsemen

The Norsemen were essentially a maritime people. They found fame and plunder on the seas. They harried Scotland

and founded colonies in the Orkneys, the inner and Outer Hebrides and Northern Ireland. It was inevitable that they would eventually disembark on the Isle of Man and disrupt its peace.

What is thought to be the earliest recorded attack on Mann occurred in 798 when the Vikings landed on the islet off Peel. By the end of the 9th Century there were Viking settlers and the Island became a pawn in the fight between Ireland and the Kings of Scandinavia.

The historical records of this time are obscure, but a character from this period has formed a great part of early Manx history. Though his identity is disputed, 'King Orry' is attributed with establishing three important bulwarks of Manx society – the State, a legislative body and a standing army. The record of the Monks of Rushen Abbey, near Castletown, the 'Chronicum Manniae' favours the Viking King, Godred Crovan, son of Harald the Black of Iceland, as the real 'King Orry'. He reached Mann in 1075 but was heavily defeated by the inhabitants. He returned again with a strengthened army and landed in Ramsey Bay. Legend has it that, on landing he looked at the Milky Way which shone bright that night, and declared "There is my path, running from my country to this place" or words to that effect. Ever since, the Manx have called the Milky Way 'Yn Rad Mooar Ree Goree" ("the great track of King Orry"). Whatever, he was sufficiently fortified to defeat the Manx on this occasion, in battle on Skyhill. He spared his vanquished opponents and ruled for 16 years. The name of King Orry is still much loved and used on the Island.

Godred Crovan established the Kingdom of Mann and the Isles and with him begins the real recorded history of the Island. There are two important 'ship burial' excavations on the Island, at Knock-y-Dooney, near Kirk Andreas, and at Balladoole, in Kirk Arbory, which date from this time. Chiefs were buried in this way. Their ship was drawn ashore and equipped with everything that they might need for the 'journey to Odin', including his sword, spear, fishing gear, a bowl and a sacrificial knife.

Cregneash

The second Scandinavian period, started by Godred Crovan lasted from 1079 to 1266. It is a period of great importance for the development of the Manx system of government. Godred ruled the British islands, from Dublin and Leinster to the Isle of Lewis. His descendants were to rule Mann for nearly two hundred years. At various times, the Kings lived in Dublin, Northumbria and Mann. During the transition period from warriors of the seas to landowners and farmers, the Vikings left the Celts to run the farms and harvest the crops whilst they traded with the adjacent islands, Iceland and the South of Europe.

The Cistercian Abbey of St Mary was built and constituted at Rushen Abbey during this period. It quickly became a source of great power in the Island and was a huge influence on the lives of the islanders. Another important development near the end

Castletown

of this period was the tying of the Island's fortunes to the English crown. Reginald, a tough Viking who, the sagas say, spent three years continually at sea, was desperate to hold on to Mann as part of his kingdom. In his anxiety, he swore to be a liegeman to Henry III of England, in return for 2 hogsheads of wine and 120 crannocks of corn.

The Scandinavian influences have stood the test of time and still appear in a multitude of ways in everyday life in the Island. The most marked features are the land tenure system, the legislature and the diocese of Sodor and Mann, all of which differ greatly from their counterparts in Great Britain. There are many words of Scandinavian extraction including Snaefell, the Island's highest peak, which means 'Snow Mountain'. The Norse settlers used "by" as the ending to many of their words and this remains a feature in many place names. Kirby meaning Church farm, Colby meaning Kolli's farm, Jurby as Ivar's farm, and Sulby are a few examples.

Monks and Bishops

Although the Vikings eventually became Christians, it was not before they had extinguished the light of Christianity, which had burned brightly on Mann from the fourth century onwards. Around the beginning of the eleventh century the Manx began, once again, to embrace Christianity. From the time of the founding of Rushen Abbey by the Cistercians of Furness Abbey in Barrow, it is possible to get a clearer picture of developments from the writings of the monks.

The Manx bishops are known as the Bishops of Sodor and Man, and the earliest reference to the Diocese of Sodor and Man seems to be in 1154. Consisting of the southern islands of Scotland, it extended from the Hebrides to Arran and the Isle of Man itself. Sodor owes its derivation from two Norse words meaning southern isles, so in fact Sodor and Man means "The southern Isles and Man".

Bishops have always played an important role in the history of the Island, sometimes leading the people by good example, at other times abusing their power and privileged position. In 1266 the connection between the "Isles and Sodor" came to an end, although the diocese continued to be under the rule of a distant Norwegian Archbishop until the fifteenth century. It was during this period the Island was divided into parishes.

After Norse rule had come to an end, the Isle of Man was the subject of many struggles, which saw its ownership passing between the Scots and the English. It was not until 1346 that the Island came firmly and finally under English rule. During this period immediately before the long reign of the Stanleys, the Island's people suffered grievously. Contemporary writings of the time report that the Island was "desolate and full of wretchedness". In another report the writer told of a great battle on the slopes of South Barrule, in which some Irish freebooters who plundered everything of value heavily defeated the Manx. Only the purchase of corn from Ireland saved the people from starvation. So poor were the Islanders that they could no longer afford to make any more of the magnificent crosses for which they had been renowned in earlier times.

The Stanleys

The Stanley dynasty ruled the Isle of Man from 1405 – 1736. The first King of Man, Sir John Stanley I, never came to the Island and was succeeded by his son Sir John Stanley II, a wise but somewhat despotic ruler, who at least conferred some benefits on the people. It is recorded that there were two revolts against his authority. To prevent a repetition, he increased the power of the governors and substituted trial by battle with

Peel Castle

trial by jury as a means of settling disputes. Many of his successors did not visit their kingdom, and those who did come often only paid a fleeting visit.

The next major turning point in the story of Mann came with the arrival of James Stanley, the 7th Earl of Derby. In 1643 James, or as the Manx people called him, 'Yn Stanlagh Mooar' ('The Great Stanley'), was ordered by King Charles I of England to go to the Isle of Man and put down a threatened revolt by the Manx. Hiding an iron hand in a velvet glove he soon made himself popular. Although the people of this period enjoyed the peace, they had less liberty.

Illiam Dhone

With Charles II on the throne of England, Yn Stanlagh Mooar proved his loyalty once more to the Crown and threw in his lot with the Royalists. Leading his troops, three hundred Manxmen amongst them, he set off in support of the King, but Stanley was defeated and executed. At this time, the great Manx patriot William Christian or 'Illiam Dhone' as the Manx knew him, anticipated punitive action against the Islanders and gathered together the people at Ronaldsway to assess the future. He ordered the militia to capture all military installations. Everything was captured, including Peel and Rushen castles, which were soon given up by Stanley's widow, and the Island eventually surrendered to the Parliamentarians.

William Christian paid a terrible price for his actions. After the Restoration and some ten years after leading the revolt against the Countess of Derby, Illiam Dhone was shot to death on Hango Hill at Castletown.

The Atholls', the Smuggling Trade, Decay and the British Crown

The 18th Century was a turbulent period

for the Manx. The end of rule by the Stanleys, serious disputes with the English Parliament, and the destruction of the smuggling trade (the only way the Island had been financially kept afloat) all caused unrest. The period also saw the passing of The Act of Settlement was passed in 1704, effectively the Island's Magna Carta, and in 1736 under the rule of the 2nd Duke of Atholl, the Manx Bill of Rights was introduced. This Act in effect did away with despotic government and replaced it with an oligarchic government - the Keys or the Lower House of Tynwald. Constitutional Government was just around the corner.

Working hard for the people over half a century during this era was the much-loved Bishop Thomas Wilson. Bishop of Sodor and Man for 58 years. He fed the populace in times of crop failure, promoted education, established schools and libraries around the Island, and laboured long on behalf of the Manx State.

On the 11th July 1765 the Island passed into the ownership of the British Crown. As the Manx standard was lowered at Castle Rushen and the Union flag raised, George III was proclaimed King of Man. John the 3rd Duke of Atholl had sold the Island to the Imperial Parliament for £70,000. The prosperity of the Island, such as it was, disappeared overnight with the demise of the smuggling trade and London appeared well satisfied. This was not to be the end of the Atholl connections with the Isle of Man.

As the Island fell into decay and its people into despair, the Government in London felt obliged to try and rectify this parlous state of affairs and in 1793 appointed the 4th Duke of Atholl to be Governor. This appointment was not a success and in 1829 he severed his relationship with the Island for the sum of £417,000 and left.

George IV, King of Great Britain and Ireland, became Lord of Man. The period immediately after the Duke's departure saw little change. London continued to control the Island's revenue, and the House of Keys still largely ignored the peoples' wishes by electing one of their "own" whenever a vacancy in the House occurred. Help was at hand though in the form of Mr. Henry Loch, later to be Lord Loch and after whom part of Douglas Promenade is named.

Appointed as Governor in 1863, Henry Loch brought energy and a real sense of purpose to the position. Working closely with Tynwald Court, lengthy negotiations with Her Britannic Majesty's Government were eventually concluded in 1866 to ensure that after the running expenses of the Manx Government were met, any surpluses could be retained on the Isle of Man for improvements to a fledgling infrastructure. Part of the agreement called for the House of Keys to be popularly elected and for the English Government to receive a sum of £10,000 annually from insular revenue as a contribution towards the defence of the Realm, a payment that, although much increased, continues to this very day.

Early Tourism

Even before the arrival of Governor Loch, the Island had started to become popular as a tourist destination. Certainly with more and more of the revenue being retained locally and spent on improving the infrastructure, it was not too long before the population increased and communications to and from the Island vastly improved. Towards the end of the 1800's as the railways and their associated shipping companies opened up the adjacent islands to travel for all, tourism in the Isle of Man mushroomed. Much of the infrastructure that exists today owes its initial development to this period. Hotels, trains, piers, theatres, reservoirs, steamships and roads all played their part in thrusting the Island to the forefront of the domestic British leisure market.

As the new post-Victorian era arrived, the Island rose to the challenge of mass tourism and for decades happily served the Lancashire cotton workers, the Yorkshire miners, Scottish engineers, Geordie ship builders and a whole host of other folk and their families as they sought their annual escape from a life of hard work. During the twentieth century the Isle of Man, like many other places around the world, has witnessed change to its economy. As the old and traditional industries declined, new methods of sustaining the population arose; as our motto says, 'Quocunque Jeceris Stabit' – 'Which Ever Way You Throw Me I Will Stand'. Investment in tourism continues. What has never changed though, is the traditional Manx welcome offered to our visitors. Please enjoy our Island as much as we enjoy your visiting us.

Douglas

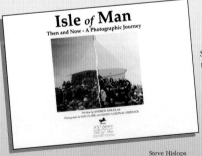

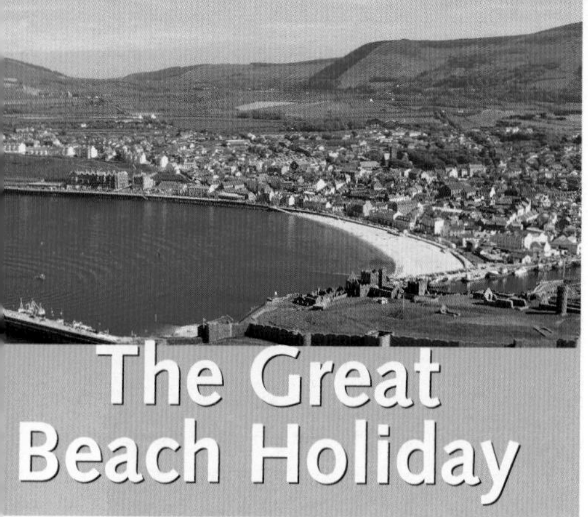

The Great Beach Holiday

With over 100 miles of coastline, it is not surprising that there are great beaches on the Island. What is perhaps, more unlikely is the fantastic variety of them. For sandcastle enthusiasts the choice beaches are in the south, but for the beachcomber looking for long deserted stretches, head to the north. Remember to consider the direction of the wind before setting out as, in the summer, a strong breeze off the Irish Sea can make beaches on one side of the Island feel arctic while the other side may be glorying in Mediterranean sunshine. Most beaches are safe, but do beware of the strong currents that circle the Island a short distance off shore, particularly around the Point of Ayre and the Calf Sound.

The Government owns all the beaches, up to the high water mark and there are no charges for their use. On beaches away from the towns, facilities may be scarce, so take with you what you need, and, of course, take it away again. Some remoter beaches are tricky to get to, so be prepared.

The beaches listed in this section run from Port St Mary round the Island clockwise.

Port St Mary

The beach at Port St Mary is a splendid semi-circular sweep of golden sand. Behind is a stone wall, above which is a classic Victorian sea front, covered in flags and at night, lit up by coloured light bulbs. The beach is very clean, swimming is safe and it is a great place for a day out with the kids. The town has all the amenities and the pretty harbour, which is full of yachts, has a good pub.

Port Erin

Between the breakwater and the dramatic Bradda Head at Port Erin, there is another perfect stretch of golden sand. This is a notably safe beach and a stream bisects it, which is a magnet for kids with their buckets and spades. Again, the town has all the facilities that you need. On a fine summer's evening, this is a place to linger, as the sunsets can be stunning. If you need a break from the sand castle business, the walk up Bradda Head provides great views back over the town and north along the wild stretch of coastline towards Peel.

Fleshwick Bay

This small stony beach is far from comfortable, but if you are after seclusion, it can be a great spot for a quiet afternoon. And if you want something more strenuous, the walks up the steep hills either side of the tiny bay take you on to dramatic cliffs. 'Fleshwick' is derived from a Scandinavian word and means 'green creek'. The steep slate cliffs on either side provide excellent shelter from all winds except the northerlies.

Enjoying the fun of the beach

Niarbyl

This small stony beach is a favourite with families because of the rock pools. There is a car park at the end of the road down from Dalby and access to the beach from there is straightforward. A short distance along the coastal footpath, below Cregganmoar, is another beach, the White beach also known among locals as the Secret beach. There is a small sandy beach at low tide and there is a stream. It is usually quiet.

Glen Maye

The beach below the village of Glen Maye is small and rocky and the best reason to stroll through the glen, down to it, is to walk off a good lunch at the Waterfall, the honest pub by the car park.

Peel

Experts note that the sand on Peel beach is not the good binding stuff and to build your epic Transylvanian castle here will take incredible perseverance. Nonetheless, Peel beach is a fine curve shaped stretch with the harbour and red sandstone castle at one end. It can get a clattering when the wind swings in hard of the Irish Sea. Peel is the centre of what remains of the Manx fishing industry and somehow the town has escaped any major developments. It still exudes charm. The sunsets in Peel can be glorious.

The beach and in fact, the whole sea front is dominated by St Patrick's Isle, the site of the castle. No other part of the Isle of Man has played so great and interesting a part in the its history. Peel is worth visiting for this alone and a walk along the beach is a good place to view the castle from.

Glen Mooar to the Point of Ayre

Along the Northwest coast, the beach stretches unbroken for some 14 miles (22 kilometres). It is a wild and unkempt beach

Looking South from Jurby Head

and not really the place to bring the family, but if you are interested in birds, rare coastal plants or a long windy walk on your own, then it is for you.

The Ayres, between Rue Point and the Point of Ayre are of particular ecological importance and the Central Ayres is an Area of Special Scientific Interest (ASSI). For more information on this, see the 'Coast and Islands' section.

At the southern end of this stretch of beach, around Glen Mooar and Jurby Head, steep sand cliffs, which are slowly eroding, meet the beach. Walking in the shingle here can be tough going and it is much easier if the tide is out so you can walk along the sandy flats that appear. North of Jurby head, there is a footpath that weaves through the low dunes which are bound by spiny marram grass.

You may see seals along this beach, but you are more likely to come across the many birds that enjoy this habitat – little terns, oyster catchers, ringed plovers and turnstones are common.

There is access to the coast via at a few places including The Cronk, Blue Point and Rue Point. From Kirk Michael heading north, there are no villages beside the beach, so take all the supplies that you may need for your walk with you.

Ramsey

The beach from the Point of Ayre down the east coast to Ramsey is also unbroken and backed up by soft dunes the whole way. There are a couple of places where it is accessible – the Point of Ayre, Cranstal, and the Dog Mills – but in Ramsey it is broader and sandier. The stretch between the harbour and the headland approaching Port Lewaigue is wide and flat at low tide. The Queen's pier has fallen into serious disrepair and is now, sadly, closed. At low tide, you can walk all the way along to Port Lewaigue. Looking back, there are good views along the gently sweeping coast to the Point of Ayre. Swimming in Ramsey Bay is safe and there are plenty of shops and other amenities nearby.

Port Erin

Port e Vullen

There is a small stony beach here, which can be a good retreat from the wind if it is blowing out of the Southwest.

Port Mooar

There is a road that leads down to this small, rocky cove with a car park at the end. The beach is not especially exciting, but there is a great short walk, over the rocks and round the near headland, to Gob ny Portmooar. A short distance further, heading inland, will bring you up to the church at Maughold, renowned for the Celtic and Norse stone crosses in the churchyard.

Port Cornaa

From Glen Mona, you can drive all the way down to the sea at Cornaa. Again, the

Laxey

stony beach is not much to write postcards home about, but the Ballaglass river flows out here and there are some quiet pools where the swimming is very safe for children. There is a footpath back up the glen (part of the Raad ny Foillan) to Cornaa village which is a lovely wooded walk.

Laxey

When the tide is in, Laxey beach is no more than a short, steep stony shelf. But at low tide, there is a wedge of soft sand and rock pools. There is a good café right on the beach and shops nearby.

Douglas

Douglas Bay was once a great Victorian beach. It may look a little forlorn today, but it retains some of its grandeur. The sweeping promenade of Victorian boarding houses is a great sight, and best appreciated from the top of Douglas Head. It stretches for almost 3 kilometres (2 miles) and is built on reclaimed beach

Castletown was the capital of the Isle of Man until 1869 when Douglas surpassed it because of its deep water harbour, which you have to cross to climb the headland. The rise of the Steam Packet Company coincided with development of the harbour, and together they did much to improve legitimate trade with England and dampen rumours that the Island was a smuggler's paradise.

The beach at Douglas has sandy parts and stretches of shingle, rock pools and large beds of seaweed. It is over 2 kilometres (1 1/4 miles) long and, even on a hot summer's day, there is always room for everyone. That said, it is more capacious when the tide is out. There are plenty of cafes and pubs along the prom, as well as shops and other amenities close by.

Derbyhaven

From Douglas south the coast is maritime hardcliff, which means that there are practically no beaches and those that there are small and inaccessible. The next large beach is at Derbyhaven, once developed by the Derby family into the Island's main port, on the north side of the shingle bank that connects the small Island of Langness to the mainland. There are rocks and pools spread across the beach at low tide and aircraft coming in to land at Ronaldsway Airport whirr overhead. It is not a beautiful beach, but it is often quiet and there are fine walks on Langness if you tire of shrimping.

Castletown

Castletown beach starts on the other side of the shingle bank leading to Langness and stretches all the way to the town harbour and the mouth of Silver Burn. There are long sandy patches when the tide is out. The beach faces south and can be windy. The backdrop to the beach, with King William's College at one end and Castle Rushen at the other is impressive. There is parking all along the seafront from what is called 'Hango Hill' (the site of a small ruin and near the spot where the Island's executions used to take place), to the edge of the town.

Gansey Bay

To the south of Castletown, the shoreline is covered in lava beds, with needle rocks until Poyllvaaish. There are small stretches of beach between here and Gansey Bay, where there is a long, lovely flat swath of sand, which is excellent for swimming and water sports.

Tide Information:

Tide times in the Isle of Man are based on high water Liverpool plus or minus the following differences:

Calf Sound +0.05 mins
Douglas -0.04 mins
Peel - 0.02 mins
Ramsey + 0.04 mins

Remember to add the hour for Summer Time. Tidal information can be obtained from the local press or on Manx Radio immediately following the weather forecasts.

Weather Information: Weather forecasts are broadcast regularly, particularly at news times, on Manx Radio courtesy of the Isle of Man Meteorological Office. The frequencies used for Manx Radio are 1368 kHz AM. 89-97.2-103.7 MHz Stereo FM. Shipping Forecasts are broadcast daily by BBC Radio 4 (long wave 198 kHz 1515 M) at 05.55, 13.55, 17.50 and 00.33. Weather Forecasts are broadcast by BBC Radio 4 at 06.03, 06.55, 07.55, 08.58, 12.55, 17.55, 21.59 and 00.20. For further information on weather and tides in the Isle of Man, please contact the local Harbour Master in your area or Douglas Harbour Control on (01624) 686628.

View of the beach at Peel from the castle

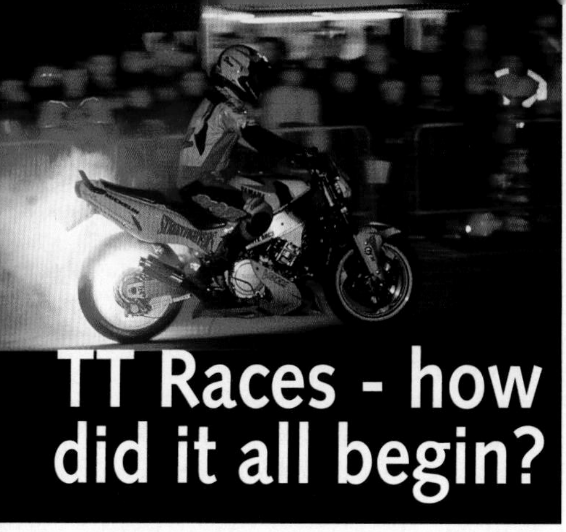

TT Races - how did it all begin?

It is hard to realise in this day and age, that the most famous motorcycle races in the world had their beginnings in 1897 in Paris. James Gordon Bennett, an American, had been sent there by his father to set up a continental edition of the family newspaper, the New York Herald. On arriving in the French capital, Gordon Bennett Jnr quickly embraced the European way of life and was soon enjoying a passionate love affair with the automobile, which led him on to becoming a founder member of the French Automobile Club. In turn he proposed, in 1900, the Gordon Bennett Cup for automobile racing which led on to the foundation of the TT Races.

In the first few years of the twentieth century British manufacturing was going through a crisis. The glory of the Victorian era had gone and a mood of despondency, stagnation and lack of direction lay over the land. Across the Channel, the Continentals were enjoying a revival. No regressive Government placing restrictions on the automobile. Every encouragement was being given to the fledgling manufacturers and they were soon producing machines capable of travelling at one mile a minute, whilst in Britain there was a ridiculous speed limit of 14 miles per hour and in effect, a ban on racing.

The British flame of inventiveness, whilst at times allowed to burn to a dangerously low level, is never quite extinguished ... and so it was, that after casting envious eyes at the achievements of their "Continental Cousins" ... a movement began, through the efforts of the Automobile Club of Great Britain and Ireland, to bring about change. There was still a long way to go, and in the meantime such was the crushing superiority of the Continentals, in particular the French, that it hardly seemed worthwhile for the British to enter races ... but they persisted and in 1902 they won! S.F.Edge of England, driving the much improved Napier, won when he was the only driver to complete the 351.5 mile course between Paris and Innsbruck in Austria.

As it had been decided that the winning nation would host the following year's event, there was more than a little concern that Great Britain would be unable to fulfil its obligation. England fretted, whilst Ireland did something about it! The Irish, spotting that the name of the sponsoring organisation was the Automobile Club of Great Britain and Ireland, moved quickly and passed an Act which brought racing on public roads in the Emerald Isle into being and secured the immediate future of the series. The 1903 race, over a distance of 327.5 miles, featuring several laps of a figure of eight circuit around Athy in County Kildare was not a success for the English team, the race being won by the German driver Jenatzy.

Interest in the Race was increasing but racing on the highways and by-ways of Britain was still impossible, in fact in 1903 a 20 m.p.h. speed restriction had been introduced. National pride and the future development of the British automobile industry was at stake. Into the breach stepped Julian Orde, later to become Sir Julian Orde. This far sighted gentleman had an ace up his sleeve ... his cousin, Lord Raglan was the Governor of the Isle of Man. Julian Orde reasoned correctly that this small Island, with its own Parliament and a fledgling tourist industry might well be the place to offer the British automobile industry

TT in full action

a home and a chance to hold the eliminating trials for the Gordon Bennett International Races.

Shortly after the French won the 1904 Race in Germany, it became obvious that arrangements were not up to the mark for the 1905 Race and the first suggestions of a more permanent home for the series were beginning to surface. Julian Orde returned to the Island in the spring of 1905 with various suggestions to ensure the future of the Race; the Island's politicians and people were enthusiastic. The imagination of the British public was captured and the clamour for a permanent home within easy reach of the masses began to reach fever pitch. Meanwhile the French smugly sat back and showed a singular lack of concern, to this almost impertinent challenge to their supremacy. The appropriate Act was passed through Tynwald, the Manx Parliament, and the rest as they say, is history!

But what of the motorcycle? The landmark event of the year 1905 was a motorcycle trial, to be held on the 31st May, immediately after the Gordon Bennett trials. The Trial was held under the auspices of the Auto-Cycle Club, the forerunner to the Auto-Cycle Union and was brought about in response from a desire to challenge the French still further. Alas in 1906 no motorcycle trials took place, but by the January of 1907 an atmosphere of determination existed and in response to a suggestion by the editor of "The Motor Cycle" to run a competition on similar lines to the car TT, bore fruit. The first race took place on the 28th May 1928 with a field of nineteen competitors. It was a success and over the succeeding decades the Isle of Man and its people have built up the TT Races into a marvellous fortnight long festival, dedicated to the two and three-wheeled sport.

Winner of the senior TT 1999 race - David Jefferies

Throughout the history of the races there has always been a tradition of riders who have mastered the tricky 37 3/4 mile road racing circuit with consummate skill. It is a demanding course, requiring absolute concentration and an almost photographic memory of the course ... and those riders who can combine those skills with an ability to become as one with their machine, tend to stand above all the other marvellous competitors. Memories of the great riders and their achievements are legion and the mere mention of legendary names such as Stanley Woods, Geoff Duke, Mike Hailwood and Joey Dunlop provokes animated discussion as to who really was the "best". Well in all honesty, anyone who competes in the TT or the amateur Grand Prix races has to be just that little bit "special".

In 1999 there were twenty countries represented and together with seven lady competitors, all was set fair for the 88th year of racing on the mountain circuit. Fans were not to be disappointed. Some of the racing statistics are breathtaking. With almost 145,000 miles of practice and racing covered in the 1999 festival, the riders tackled a course that starts in Douglas, takes them around the Island's roads ... and hundreds of gear changes later, usually over a 3, 4 or 6 laps race brings them back to the capital having covered every type of road condition imaginable. Up hill and down dale, from just a couple of feet above sea level in Ramsey, to Hailwood Height at almost 1400 feet above sea level everything is there for rider and spectator alike. In 1999 Jim Moodie on the on his first lap of the Senior TT set a new absolute lap record for the course at 124.45 mph, with a time of 18 minutes 11.4 seconds. Breathtaking!

Each year riders and supporters from all corners of the world travel to the Island to compete and take part in this internationally renowned event, but it just does not continue because of a quirk of fate at the beginning of the twentieth century. It continues because the people of the Island and their Government want it to happen. Where else would you find a population ready and willing to provide up to fifteen hundred marshals, trained first aiders, scrutineers and where the scoreboards are operated by cubs and scouts as young as ten years of age. The TT races are something special and are not to be missed!

ISLE OF MAN

The Isle of Man has something to offer everyone, with some 224 square miles of some of the most spectacular scenery around. The past is brought to life with a number of award winning heritage centres, museums and ancient castles some of which can be accessed on vintage transport, including Steam and Electric Railways, even horse drawn trams.

Golf, Angling, Rambling, Sailing and Pony Trekking are just some of the activities the island has to offer, and a wide range of Events and Attractions are available throughout the year to suit all tastes.

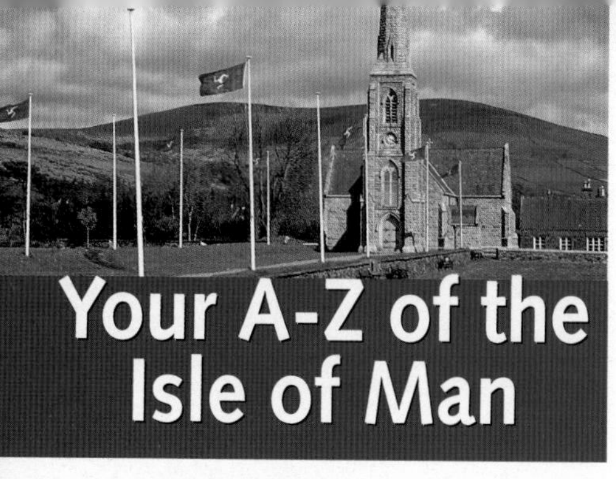

Your A-Z of the Isle of Man

Ballasalla

Distances: Castletown 3m, Douglas 9m, Laxey 17m, Peel 10m, Port Erin 6m, Port St Mary 7m, Ramsey 24m.

Ballasalla lies in the parish of Malew within the Sheading of Rushen. Flowing gently through the area is the Silverburn river and it is from this river that the village received its name. It is probable that Salla or Sallach was the ancient Gaelic name by which the early inhabitants knew the river; translated into English it means "the village of the sally or willow river". A more modern Gaelic translation of Silverburn is Awin Argid or Silver River.

The village is served by a regular bus service but during the summer months travelling by steam train is the way to get to the village. The line to Ballasalla was built in 1873-74, connecting Douglas and Port Erin. In 1986 a new station was built in Ballasalla, the first on the Island in almost a century.

Within Ballasalla's boundaries lie the ruins of the Cistercian Rushen Abbey, said to have been founded in 1098 by Magnus, King of Norway. The building of the abbey commenced in 1134 and although, as with many ancient sites, it was utilised over the centuries as a ready made source of building materials, much of the original buildings remain.

Records show that a number of kings and abbots lie buried within the abbey's precincts, and an excavation in the early part of this century discovered a skeleton of a man buried with a bronze figure representing the Egyptian God Osiris, which points to him having been a Crusader. The 'Chronicon Manniae', ('Chronicles of Mann'), a valuable reference work for the early history of the Island, were written at Rushen Abbey. Contained within the chronicles is an account of the murder by a knight called Ivar of Reginald II, King of Mann.

The monks were busy in other areas as well, draining the land, straightening the course of the local rivers and streams, and generally influencing the local way of life. One example of their work can be seen a few yards upstream from the Abbey Gardens. Known as the Monk's Bridge, its Gaelic name was Crossag, the little cross or crossing, it still carries people over the Silverburn river. Dating from the twelfth century and only 3½ feet wide, it is one of the finest examples of a packhorse bridge to be found anywhere in the British Isles.

Just a little further upstream from the bridge, the Silverburn is joined by the Awin Ruy, or Red River, whose bed is strewn with boulders as it flows down from Rozefel, Granite Mountain. Nowadays this mountain is called Stoney Mountain and it was from this source that much of the building materials came for the building of the new Douglas Breakwater in 1979.

The Norsemen who named the mountain also recognised the colouring of the granite as it was exposed to the elements and knew it as Rjoofjall, Ruddy Mountain. On the short walk from the abbey to Silverdale Glen also look out for the Wishing Well.

Silverdale was originally the site of the Creg Mill - its dam is now used as a boating lake. The water wheel here was developed by the ingenious use one of the old Foxdale mine's water wheels. The café here is open all day throughout the season.

Ronaldsway Airport falls within Ballasalla's boundaries. Ronaldsway lies a little to the south of the village and can be

Your A-Z of the Isle of Man

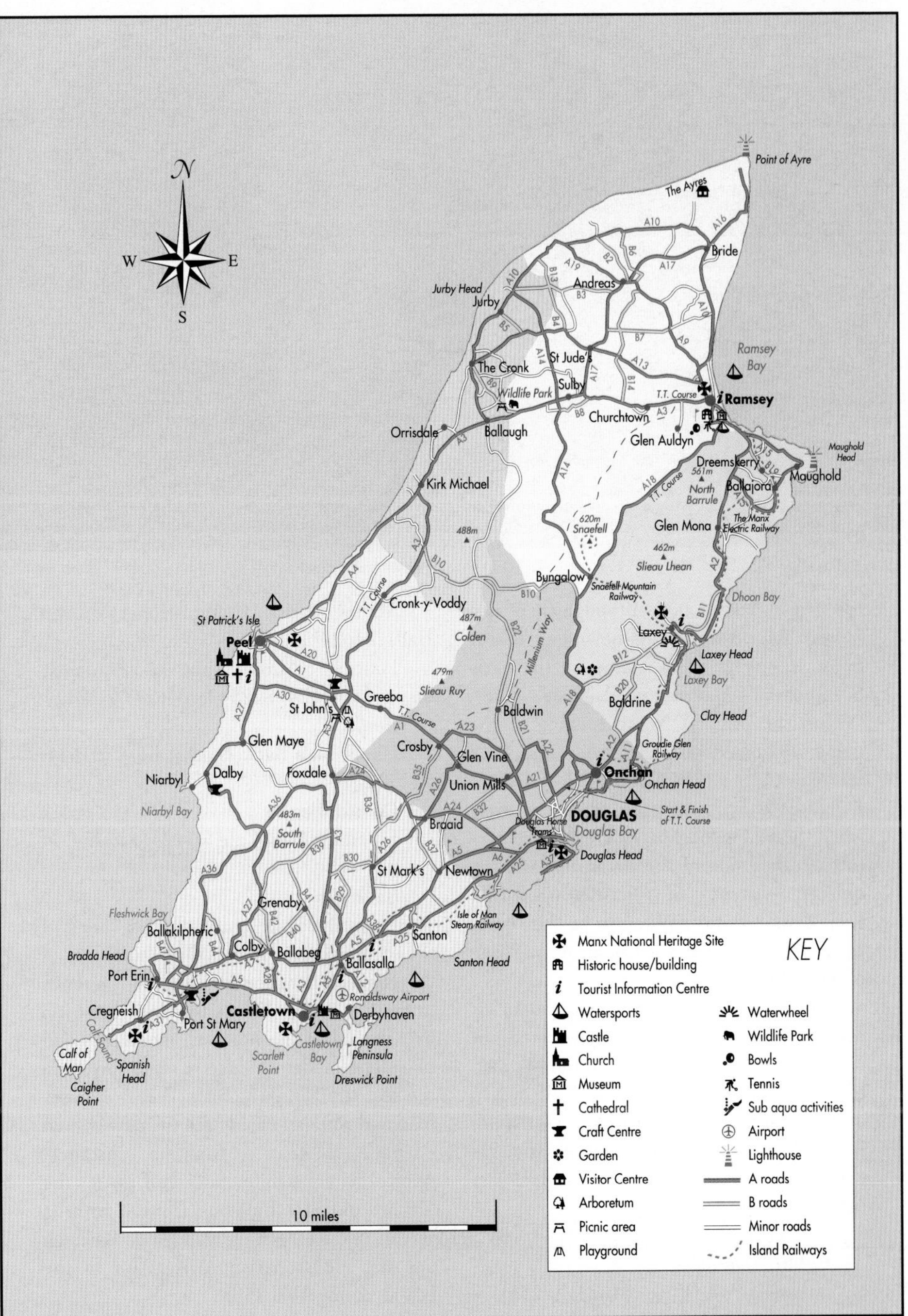

Ballasalla

reached by bus or taxi. Although there is a railway halt nearby, this is now rarely if ever used. It was given its name by the early Scandinavians and means "Reginald's Ford". Within the original Norse spelling of the name, Rognvaldsvao, the vao would have referred to the tarbet across the neck of Langness which was used as the pathway when the Viking longboats were dragged over to the other side of the peninsula and the quieter waters of Castletown Bay. Ronaldsway is also reputed to be the site of King Orry's castle and it has been the scene of many battles.

After the execution of Illiam Dhone, his estate of Ronaldsway was sequestrated but later returned to his family, and the last man to include Ronaldsway in his title was a direct descendant of William Christian, Rear-Admiral Sir Hugh Christian who was elevated to the peerage but who died just before the patent reached him.

Public Amenities

Ballasalla Post Office (01624) 822531

Malew Parish Commissioners (Town Hall) (01624) 823522

Police Station (not continuously manned) (01624) 822543, (01624) 631212

Banks

Isle of Man Bank, Station Road (01624) 822503

Leisure Centre

Silverdale Glen Cafe (01624) 823474

Ballaugh

Ballaugh village marks the beginning of the scenery that is so typical of this corner of the Island, where the lonely glens run down to the low sandy cliffs of the shore against a background of the northern mountains and hills. The modern village is some way from the sea, straddling the main Peel to Ramsey road and you can clearly see the new church - built 1832 – from a distance. Approximately a mile and a half nearer the sea lies old Kirk Ballaugh Church with its very distinctive "leaning" gate posts. Ballaugh has the oldest parish register on in the Island, dating from 1598.

Castletown

Distances: Ballasalla 3m, Douglas 9m, Laxey 20m, Peel 13m, Ramsey 26m, Port Erin 5m, Port St Mary 7m.

The ancient Capital of Mann for several centuries, Castletown has a charm all of its own. Sited at the edge of a long extinct and almost untraceable volcano, the town was guardian for the Manx in times of war and peace. The virtual end to commercial seaborne traffic came in the 1970's but in more recent times there has been a revival in business, with a number of commercial activities based on the finance sector being located here. In the summer the town hosts one of the Island's two agricultural shows.

Castletown is the only town in the parish of Malew and as a result of long association with the seat of government, there are many anglicised names in the vicinity. Names to look out for are Bowling Green, Great Meadow, Paradise (now Ellerslie and the former home of General Cuming who was with Wolfe at Quebec), Red Gap, Witches Mill and the Rope Walk. Many of the homestead names in the proximity such as Grenaby, Tosaby and Orrisdale indicate that Castletown and its surrounding area were once well colonised by Norsemen.

There is a regular bus service year-round to Castletown and the steam railway operates in both directions several times a day during the summer. Routes to the town are well signposted if travelling by car, although the narrow streets aren't ideal for driving.

The Silverburn gently empties into the town's picturesque harbour, flowing under the Apostles Bridge. The Dumb River enters the sea just on the western edge of the town at Red Gap. The name comes from the fact that the river makes no sound as it flows across flat country throughout its entire course.

Castletown

Castletown's Nautical Museum is well worth a visit, the main exhibit being the eighteenth century armed yacht "The Peggy", still in her original boathouse and only rediscovered by accident in 1935, a hundred years after the death of her owner Captain George Quayle.

Castletown harbour is built on a shelf of lava, clearly seen at low water. A walk along the shoreline towards Scarlett Point will show you signs of past volcanic activity. Wind, tide and rain over the aeons have exposed the volcano's surviving plug. Close by there is a Nature Trail and Visitors Centre (Open Tuesdays to Sundays 2 - 5pm, mid May until mid September).

Practically all the ancient buildings in the town are grouped around the harbour and to the seaward side of the castle. These include Castletown Grammar School, built originally as the ancient capital's first church

Castle Rushen

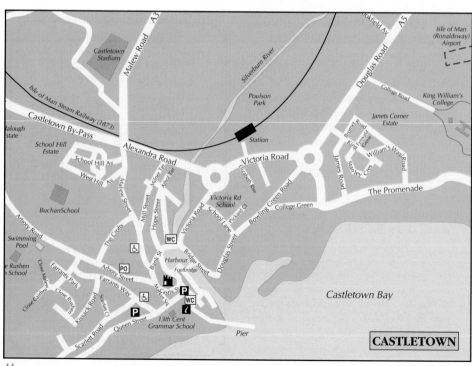

CASTLETOWN
Castletown Stadium
Malew Road A3
Silverburn River
Douglas Road A5
Isle of Man (Ronaldsway) Airport
Isle of Man Steam Railway (1873)
Castletown By-Pass
Poulson Park
College Road
King William's College
Janets Corner Estate
School Hill Estate
School Hill Av
West Hill Av
Alexandra Road
Station
Victoria Road
Elizabeth Rise
Bromet Road
Tynwald Grove
King William's Way Road
Stanley Cres
James Road
The Promenade
Malew Street
Milner Ter
Athol Ter
Mill Street
Hope Street
Victoria Rd School
Victoria Road
School Lane
Pickard Cl
Bowling Green Road
College Green
BuchanSchool
Arbory Road
Swimming Pool
The Crofts
Harbour
Bridge Street
Footbridge
Douglas Street
Bank St
Arbory Street
Farrants Park
Farrants Way
Close Malew
Close Caitbre
Close Rushen
Kissack Road
Scarlett Cl
Castle St
Market Sq
Queen Street
13th Cent Grammar School
Scarlett Road
Pier
Castletown Bay

in approximately 1200. Nearby is the old garrison church of St. Mary's built in 1826 to replace Bishop Wilson's church of 1698, saved in recent times from dereliction and now a thriving business house. On his first visit to the Island in 1777 John Wesley, the founder of Methodism preached in front of the castle and noted in his journal of the 30th June, that "A more loving, simple-hearted people than this I never saw".

A walk up from the outer harbour through the narrow streets will bring you to the old House of Keys building, which from 1709 was the seat of government until population and commercial pressures forced the Keys to move to Douglas in 1869. The builder's receipt shows that the building was constructed for the princely sum of £83-5s-6½d!

Standing sentinel over Castletown and the southern lowlands is Castle Rushen. Dating from Norse times, its huge limestone structure is visible for miles around. This imposing fortress is one of the most complete of its type in the whole of the British Isles. The staircases at Castle Rushen spiral to the right, thus forcing any attackers to use their left hand to grip their swords whilst the defenders were free to use their right hand. The castle is decorated in authentic style, and gives you a good impression of life in medieval/ seventeenth century Manxland. It is still a working castle hosting High and Low courts and at regular intervals witnessing weddings within the precincts of its courthouse.

The market square is little changed since the 1800's. In the centre of the square stands Smelt's Memorial, erected in 1838 to honour Governor Cornelius Smelt (1805 to 1832) - and to this day still incomplete. The people of Castletown refused to contribute for a statue to grace the column and for the first few years after it was erected it became known as the "Castletown Candlestick". Today it does a fine job as a traffic roundabout ... have a look at the plaque on the side, you may find it interesting.

Across from the Smelt Memorial and close to the George Hotel, is the former home of Captain John Quilliam RN who fought at the Battle of Trafalgar and saved HMS Victory from destruction by rigging a jury (temporary) rudder at the height of the fighting.

Looking down on the square is a clock presented to the Island by Queen Elizabeth I. It has only ever had one finger and is still going strong after four hundred years.

The outskirts of Castletown have almost as much history as the town itself. Lying to the east of the old metropolis is King William's College, a long time site of public school education, its great central tower dominating the landscape. The idea for a college probably first surfaced in a letter from the seventh Earl of Derby, Yn Stanlagh Mooar, to his son Charles but due to the subsequent outbreak of the English Civil War, nothing actually came to fruition until 1833. Facing the school is Hango Hill, where

Castletown

Taking on coal at Douglas

Illiam Dhone met his end. The Norse name for the hill was Hangaholl, or Hill of Hanging, and William Christian was the last person to be executed there. It is also a very important archeological site. The ruins are in fact of a blockhouse built by the seventh Earl at the time of the unrest in England.

To the west of the town is the Balladoole estate centred on the fine Balladoole House, the home of the Stevensons for many hundreds of years. There is evidence in the Manx Museum that at least six generations of the family lived on the estate prior to a mention in the manorial records of 1511. John Stevenson was the Speaker of the House of Keys from 1704 to 1738 and he is remembered by the Manx nation for the manner in which he led the Keys in their patriotic struggle against the tenth Earl of Derby. Bishop Wilson called him "The Father of his Country" and at one time he was imprisoned in Castle Rushen for championing the rights of his fellow countrymen. The last bearer of the family name was Sir Ralph Stevenson, who retired as British Ambassador to Egypt in 1955.

To the west of Balladoole is Poyll Vaaish, which is easily reached by car, or on foot from Castletown by following the coastal footpath Raad ny Foillan. There are superb views of the surrounding countryside, especially the panorama northwards as the low hills of the coastal areas roll ever upwards to the central mountain range, with Snaefell visible in the far distance.

Just after dropping down from the basaltic Stack of Scarlett you will come upon a small quarry which produces high quality black marble. It was from this source that Bishop Wilson gifted the stone from which the steps of St. Paul's Cathedral were made, and again in recent years replaced when worn out. Close by the Stevenson's ancestral home there is the site of a Viking ship burial mound and this together with a number of important archeological sites makes a visit to the area well worthwhile.

Castletown

At the point where the coastal footpath joins the main road (A5) is the area known as Poyll Vaaish or translated into the English "Death Pool" or "Bay of Death". Probably the name is derived from the black marble which comprises the sea bed in the vicinity and the ripples of lava clearly seen above the low water mark. There are legends galore about this corner of the Island - stories of shipwrecks, pirates, and looters abound.

Strandhall, which lies to the right when heading south has a spring flowing down onto the shore and legend tells that, although the source of the spring lies many feet above sea level, it is reputed to be a salt water spring with petrifying powers. Indeed, at extremely low tides and particularly after a storm has moved the sands, the remains of a large petrified forest can sometimes be seen.

Rounding Baie ny Carrickey, The Bay of the Rocks, the road follows the water's edge passing as it does the Treen lands of Kentraugh, "Shore End", the home of the Gawne family for centuries. There are fine sands here with excellent boating waters. At the west end of the bay lies Gansey, this Scandinavian name means Magic Bay. Peaceful now but in the past the scene of many a struggle between the forces of law and order and the farmers and fishermen of Mann. In the short distance between Castletown and Kentraugh you will have moved across three parishes, Malew, Arbory and into Rushen.

Public Amenities

Castletown Post Office (01624) 822516

Castletown Commissioners (Town Hall) (01624) 825005

Harbour Master's Office (01624) 823549

Police Station (not continuously manned) (01624) 822222, (01624) 631212

Banks

Barclays, Market Square (Central Switchboard) (01624) 684444

Isle of Man Bank, Market Square (01624) 821400

Lloyds TSB Bank, Market Square (01624) 822755

Leisure Centre

Southern Swimming Pool, Arbory Road (01624) 823930

Colby and Ballabeg

To the east of Port Erin in the flat lands of Arbory are the villages of Colby and Ballabeg. Colby, Kolli's Farm, stands at the entrance to the delightful Colby Glen. A walk up the glen takes you alongside a brook which runs its lower course through wooded glades, and higher up where the gorse is a blaze of yellow. Further up the glen again there are the remains of Keeill Catreeney and a burial ground. The ancient St Catherine's or Colby Fair used to be held here. Nearby there is Chibbyrt Catreeney, Catherine's Well, and it was said that anyone who drank from here would be afflicted with an unquenchable thirst forever.

Another fair, which still survives, is Laa Columb Killey, St Columba's Day Fair. Held in a special field in either Colby or Ballabeg at the end of June each year, it attracts people from all over the Island and gives a glimpse of country life as it used to be. Ballabeg is on the ancient quarterland and the village is named from the 1511 Manorial Roll as Begson's Farm. The area is very rural and foxgloves and wild fuchsia line the quiet sheltered lanes. (Weedkillers and pesticides are not used on the Manx hedgerows and it is still possible to see wild flowers which have disappeared from other parts of the British Isles - the lanes of Arbory and the neighbouring parishes of Malew and Rushen provide excellent examples).

The church has always played an important part in the life of the south of the Island and none more so than Kirk Arbory. Built in 1757 the present church has an oak beam supporting the roof which belonged to two previous churches. There is an inscription on the beam mentioning Thomas Radcliffe, Abbot of Rushen and it seems to refer to the Stanley crest of an Eagle and Child. The grave of Captain Quilliam of H.M.S. Victory and Trafalgar fame is in the churchyard.

Along the road from the church towards Castletown is Friary Farm. Clearly visible from the road are the remains of the Friary of Bemaken, founded by the Grey Friars in 1373. The friars were assisted in its completion by stone masons who were on the Island to do work on Castle Rushen. Employed by William de Montacute and later his son, the masons were on the move around Britain strengthening castles and fortifications between 1368 and 1374. Two Ogham stones were found on the site and are now in the Manx Museum. The stones are inscribed in the ancient Ogham script which was used in much of western Britain from the fourth/fifth century AD to the early seventh century.

Cregneash

Leaving the narrow lanes of Fistard and the Howe behind, the A31 climbs still higher up Mull Hill to the village of Cregneash. Don't worry if your map refers to it as Cregneish, the first spelling is the Gaelic form, meaning 'Rock of Ages'. The village is the oldest in the Isle of Man and part of it forms the Folk Museum run by Manx National Heritage.

The thatched cottages nestle in and around a sleepy hollow and the views of the Calf of Man and the Sound are stunning. The museum has a working farm and you may also see a thatcher at work.

Across the way from the "modern" village lies the remains of an older village. The Mull Circle, in Manx Meayl, meaning Bald or Bare Hill, dates back to the late Neolithic or early Bronze Age. Used primarily as a prehistoric burial place, it is unique in archeological terms, combining the circle form with six pairs of cists, each pair having a passage between which radiates outwards. The prehistoric village was below the circle, and hut foundations and other relics were discovered on the site.

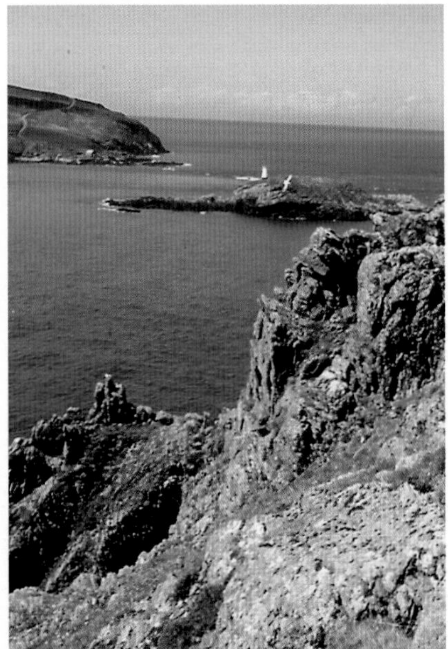
Looking towards the Sound

On the hilltop above the village is a radio beacon used by transatlantic airliners. The huddle of buildings nearby house a similar system for Irish Sea shipping. A walk on past the beacons brings you to the Spanish Head Manx National Trust area, home to the incredible chasms (See 'Mountains, Valleys Glens and Parks' for more details).

Just down the hill the Sound Cafe generates its own wind powered electricity. This is one of the most scenic spots on the Island, and if you have binoculars you may spot basking sharks or grey seals sunbathing on Kitterland. From The Sound - the Land's End of Mann – try the walk back to Port St Mary or on to Port Erin, it is well worth it.

Derbyhaven

Derbyhaven is a picturesque hamlet best reached by car - there is an occasional bus service but you'll need to check with Manx National Transport for details. Well utilised by small boats, the hamlet no longer has any commercial shipping activities, but at the time of the Vikings and their medieval successors, it was a thriving port.

The remains of the old smelthouse are still visible, probably dating from around 1711. It was here that Blacksmith John Wilks - two former Governors of the Bank of England are directly descended from him - made the Island's first penny coins, an action which Tynwald authenticated by making them legal tender. There is solid evidence to prove that exclusively Manx coinage was minted by one John Murrey, a merchant of Douglas in 1668, and he appears to have been the owner of the Derbyhaven Mint. Incidentally, it seems that the rate of exchange decided upon in 1709 by James II, tenth Earl of Derby, when he authorised a new issue was fourteen Manx pennies to twelve British, but by the time that the only Manx money issued under Atholl rule came on the market, the rate of exchange was only half this, in favour of the British coinage.

The sandy turf of the Langness Peninsula is home to the famous Castletown Golf Links.

Close by the ruins of the smelthouse is the 10th hole and it was here, 153 years before it was transferred to Epsom Downs in 1780, that the famous Derby horse race originated. It seems that the seventh Earl of Derby wished to encourage the breeding of Manx horses and as an incentive presented a cup to be won in open competition. One stipulation he put on the race was that only those horses that had been foaled within the Island or on the Calf of Man could be entered. The Manx horses of that period were small and very hardy, renowned for their speed, surefootedness and stamina. It may well be that prior to the Derby the only

Langness

Derbyhaven

time horses were in competition was after a wedding when the guests raced back to the bridegroom's home to claim the honour of breaking the bride-cake over the bride's head as she entered her new home!

Langness is very well known for its wildlife, especially birds – skylarks in particular, and it's often possible to see seals at Dreswick Point, the southern-most tip of the Isle of Man.

The waters here conceal jagged rocks which have claimed many lives. A short distance from the lighthouse and in line with the Herring Tower is Tharastack Gulley, where in 1853 the crew of the Plymouth schooner "Provider" perished. The bodies were buried in sight of the wreck and their burial site is marked by a nearby natural tombstone of rock carved with the vessel's name and the date of her loss.

Douglas

Distances: Ballasalla 9m, Castletown 12m, Laxey 8m, Peel 11m, Port Erin 15m, Port St Mary 16m, Ramsey 16m.

Located in the gentle curve of Douglas Bay, Douglas is a grand Victorian resort with a sweeping promenade, a busy quayside and harbour, some fine hotels and plenty of great family attractions.

The best place to see the town is from the top of Douglas Head – from here the whole of Douglas Bay, as far as Onchan Head, is spread out before you. Fringed by gardens to the front and with a backdrop of 2,036 ' high Snaefell, this is an unexpectedly impressive scene.

Douglas, once a small fishing port, became the Island's most important port and the centre of trade in salt, herring, hides, soap and beer thanks in large part to its sheltered position on the east coast.

During the 18th century it was also a centre for the 'running trade', by which merchants avoided high British tariffs on imported goods such as tea, tobacco, wine and brandy by importing them legally into the Isle of Man, paying lower taxes to the Lord of Mann, and then 'running' the goods to colleagues waiting along the shore on the British mainland, thus avoiding the higher British tariffs.

'Running' increased the wealth of the town, but in 1756 the British government brought an end to the business by purchasing the rights of the Lord of Mann so that all goods entering the Island paid British taxes. The Royal Navy and British customs officials controlled this, and the effect was a drastic drop in the wealth and living standards in the town. Interestingly, a commander of one of the revenue cutters

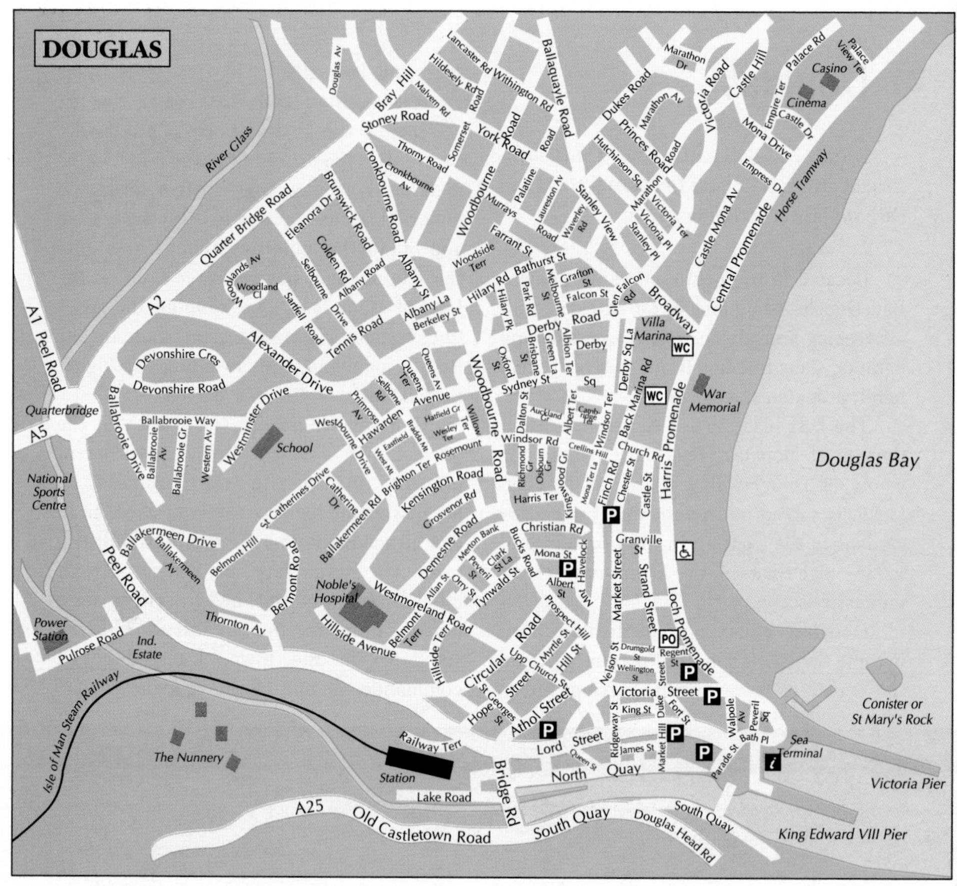

was Liet. William Bligh, later of mutiny on the 'Bounty' fame, who married a local girl, Elizabeth Betham. Peter Heywood of Douglas was also on the crew of the 'Bounty', as, of course, was Fletcher Christian whose family had strong Manx connections.

In 1801 a new pier was constructed in Douglas in the aftermath of a terrible storm in 1787 which wrecked the Island's herring fleet in a gale off Laxey. Many boats and lives were lost as they headed for the shelter of Douglas' crumbled pier.

Shipwrecks were a common feature of life for Island sailors. Sir William Hillary, who had moved to the Island after his triumphs in the Napoleonic wars, launched the appeal which led to the formation of the Royal National Lifeboat Association in 1824 after organising the rescue of 97 men from a Royal Navy cutter which had run aground in the harbour entrance in 1822.

Sir William was involved in many other rescues, including that of the paddle steamer 'St. George' in 1832 after it had become stranded on Conister Rock near the entrance to Douglas Harbour. Although a non-swimmer, Sir William took out the lifeboat with his crew and saved all 22 abroad. He was also responsible for building the Tower of Refuge on Conister Rock in 1832.

The town spread out from the harbour in the 19th century, first as Georgian residences were built for wealthy residents arrived from England and attracted by the low cost of

• BIRTHDAYS • CHOCOLATE CORNER • DASH •

CLAIRE'S • ELC • BODY SHOP • EVANS • HMV • HAWKSHEAD •

• MOTHERCARE • MILLETS • MALL CAFE •

PEACOCKS • STEAD & SIMPSON • TANDY • WYSIWYGS •

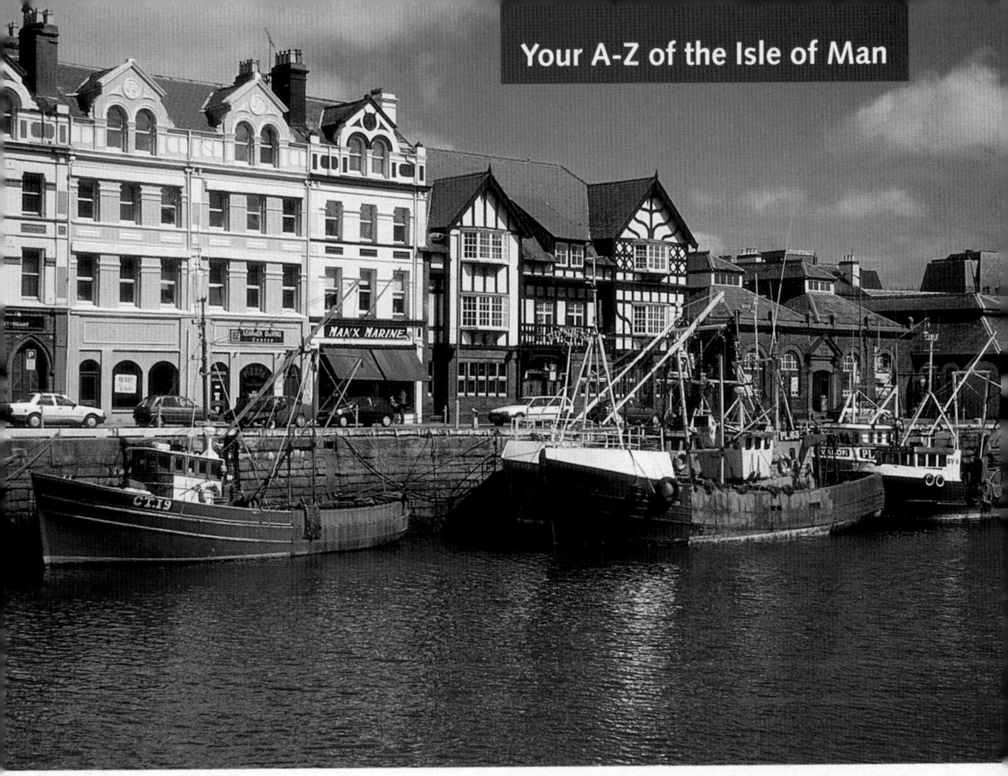

Douglas

living, and later for wealthy holiday visitors from the factory towns of northern England arriving in summer on steam ships from Liverpool and Whitehaven. A group of local businessmen got together in 1830 to build the passenger ship 'Mona's Isle' to cater for this increased traffic, and this eventually led to the formation of the Isle of Man Steam Packet Company.

Since then the town's twin piers have seen the arrival of millions of holiday makers over the decades, and today cruise ships regularly visit them. (King Edward Pier is the only public work named after the uncrowned sovereign, and at Victoria Pier the 'Dawsey' memorial commemorates David 'Dawsey' Kewley, a ropeman with the Isle of Man Steam Packet Company, who is reputed to have saved twenty four men from drowning).

Indeed, the holiday trade boomed for Douglas and the Isle of Man in the late 19th century and 20th century. From 1866 onwards Douglas took over from Castletown

Gaiety Theatre

as the Island's capital, and the latter half of the 19th century saw major developments of hotels and boarding houses, the construction of Victoria Pier in 1872 and the erection of splendid theatres and ballrooms at the same time as improving municipal facilities and housing for local residents.

Henry Bloom Noble funded the town's public baths, a park, a hospital and the Villa Marina complex in the middle of the promenade, a focus of entertainment in Douglas since 1913. The nearby Gaiety Theatre is another celebration of Douglas' Victorian/Edwardian heritage, and this provision of visitor facilities has continued into the 21st century with a whole range of entertainments from a casino, nightclubs, bars and restaurants to the towns various parks, and the superb new facilities of the National Sports Centre to the award-winning Manx Museum. The main shopping area is along Strand Street.

Douglas Town Centre

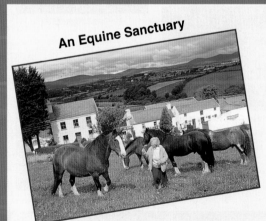

Superb location, excellent leisure facilities, Vegas style Casino and prices from only £33 It's where you want to stay*

Centrally located on the Douglas promenade, the Stakis Isle of Man Hotel & Casino boasts superb views across Douglas Bay and shore.

Situated 9 miles from the Airport, 1 mile from the sea terminal and only 1 mile away from Douglas shopping and financial area, the Hotel is multi-functional, catering for holiday makers, business travellers, social and special interest groups, conferences, meetings and functions.

On Friday and Saturday evenings the public areas of the Hotel "buzz" to the vibrant sounds of the weekend, going on into the early hours.

♦ Hotel

♦ Casino, Restaurant

♦ "Toffs" Night Club

Living Well

HEALTH CLUB - **fully equipped gymnasium, saunas, steam room, sun beds and beauty therapy room - free to residents.**

- **POOL - relax in the warm waters of our 15m pool with spa, overlooking Douglas Bay.**
- **Relax and enjoy a drink or snack at the Poolside terrace.**
- **136 well appointed bedrooms, as you would expect all with en-suite facilities, satellite TV, telephone, complimentary tea/coffee tray, trouser press and hairdryer.**
- **Whispers Bar - with music at weekends**
- **Swing Easy - themed American style restaurant and bar for casual dining.**
- **Atlantis - A la Carte restaurant in the Casino.**
- **Casino - with immediate complimentary membership for residents and non-residents. I.D. Required for non-members**
- **"Toffs" Nightclub - open until LATE (Thurs, Fri, Sat, Sun).**
- **Kursaal - Bingo Hall and 150 Vegas style slot machines.**
- **Lift to all floors, wheelchair access.**
- **Free 100 space car park.**
- ***BUSINESS* and *COMMERCIAL*.**
- ***OPEN ALL YEAR*, so where better to stay and have a meeting or conference (up to 300 delegates)**
- **Five Stakis "Assured" meeting rooms and 3 function rooms.**

♦ Swing-easy Restaurant

- **42 Non-smoking rooms.**
- **1 purpose built disabled room.**

♦ Livingwell Health Club

** ACCOMMODATION FROM £33 PER PERSON PER NIGHT BED & BREAKFAST SHARING A ROOM (SUBJECT TO AVAILABILITY) BASED ON CURRENT STAKIS HOLIDAY RATE (MINIMUM 2 NIGHTS STAY) UP TO 31/03/2000.*

For Travel Inclusive packages, our In-House Operator, **TREND TRAVEL** have **SPECIAL RATES** – call them on **01624 673275** (9.00am - 5.30pm Mon - Fri)

TRAVEL SERVICES ATOL 2267

HIGHLY COMMENDED

CENTRAL PROMENADE, DOUGLAS, ISLE OF MAN

For Hotel Reservations

TEL: 01624 662662 Fax: 01624 625535

WWW.STAKIS.CO.UK

email: reservations@stakis.co.uk

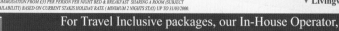

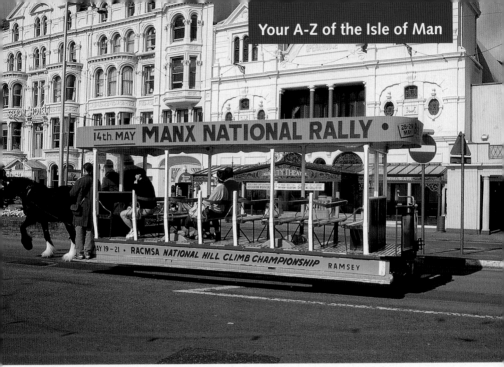

Douglas Horse Tram

In recent years Douglas has also developed as an important financial hub, dealing in international banking and insurance – with this has come the development of office blocks and facilities for these businesses, all of which ensures a vibrant future for Douglas' residents and visitors alike.

Public Amenities

Coastguard (Officer in Charge) (01624) 661664

General Post Office, Regent Street (01624) 686141

Douglas Corporation (Town Hall) (01624) 623021

Nobles (IOM) Hospital (01624) 642642

Police Station (01624) 631212

Banks

Alliance & Leicester (IOM), Prospect Hill (01624) 663566

Bank of Ireland (IOM), Christian Road (01624) 644200

Bank of Scotland (IOM), Prospect Hill (01624) 644000

Douglas Bay

Barclays, Victoria Street (01624) 684444

Isle of Man Bank, Athol St (01624) 637000

Lloyds, Prospect Hill (01624) 638000

HSBC, Ridgeway Street (01624) 684948

TSB Bank, Strand Street (01624) 673755

Building Societies

Bradford & Bingley (IOM), Ridgeway Street (01624) 661868

Britannia (IOM), Victoria Street (01624) 681100

Hailfax, Strand Street (01624) 612323

Abbey National, (01624) 644800

Nationwide Overseas, Athol Street (01624) 663494

Leisure Centres

Summerland (01624) 625511

Tourist Information

Douglas Corporation Horsetrams (01624) 675222

Harbour Control (01624) 686628

Isle of Man Railways (Steam & Electric) (01624) 663366

Isle of Man Steam Packet Company (01624) 661661

Isle of Man Transport (01624) 662525

Jersey European Airways (01624) 822162

Manx Airlines (01624) 824313

Tourist Information Centre, Sea Terminal (01624) 686801

Foxdale

Foxdale means Waterfall Dale and with the area containing many streams, it is aptly named. It was once a centre for lead mining and from the three hundred or so tons of ore that were mined each month, some fifteen to twenty ounces of silver per ton were extracted. Closed down for good in the early part of the 20th century, many of the miners emigrated to the colonies, and it has taken years for the village to begin to recover some of its lost prosperity.

Glen Maye, Dalby and Niarbyl

Glion Muigh (Glen Maye) means Yellow Glen – this is a village sitting on steep hillsides at the bottom end of the mining glens of Glen Mooar and Glen Rushen. Beyond the village the river plunges over a series of waterfalls, before finishing its dash to the sea between two hundred foot high gorse and heather clad cliffs. It is easy to see that the village of Glen Maye owes its existence to the farming and mining industries, and much of its original character has been retained.

Niarbyl, or to give it its Manx name Yn Arbyl, The Tail (on account of the long reef jutting out from the shoreline) is an ideal place for picnics, with superb views to the north and south. The isolation of this part of the Island can best be experienced from here. The full grandeur of the south western coast is clear, with the massive cliffs stretching away southward in a series of giant headlands and bays before Bradda Head briefly interrupts the flow. The Mull Hills continue the vista and from this angle it almost seems as if the Calf of Man is joined to the main Island. This is excellent walking country.

Jurby, Andreas and Bride

The three northern-most parishes of then Island fall within the Sheadings of Michael and Ayre respectively. They share virtually the same scenery and the only high ground in the area is found in the shape of the Bride Hills. Very much farming country, the northern plain is a maze of roads and lanes zigzagging between the villages. Although well signposted, it is easy to get lost, but a quick look over your shoulder towards the mountains will soon put you back on course.

Jurby in more recent times grew up around the old RAF base and, although now closed, good use is being made of the site with various small businesses based there.

Niarbyl

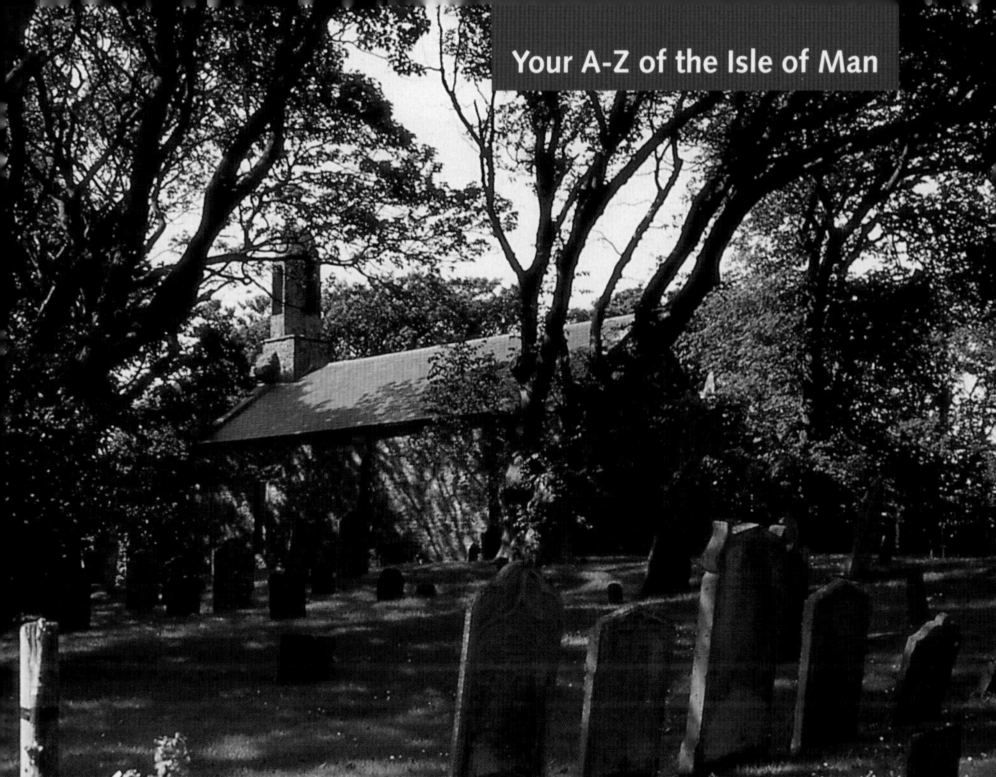

Old Ballaugh Church

The air strip is now used for motor racing events and by the local gliding club.

A visit to the old garrison church is worth a diversion and if you have time, wander through the churchyard. There is a lot of history to be imagined by reading the inscriptions on the old headstones and the church porch has a fine collection of stone crosses. In the new part of the churchyard, the well kept graves of Polish, Canadian, Anzac and British airmen are laid out in neat rows. On a clear day you can see Scotland's Mull of Galloway and its lighthouse from the back of the church.

Andreas has always been a pleasant village with a peaceful rural existence, largely uninterrupted since the end of the Viking era. In the 1940s, the land to the north and east of the village was used as a RAF base. Roads and lanes which had previously only been wide enough to suit a horse and cart were enlarged, and it was not an unusual sight to see large aircraft being manoeuvred about on the roads skirting the edge of this ancient village. In 1995 the old airfields of Andreas and Jurby were used as backdrops for the film 'The Brylcreem Boys'.

The Parish Church of Kirk Andreas with its Lombardic campanile is unexpected, but the Italian style sits well with the Manx countryside. It was built in 1802 to replace a parish church from the thirteenth century, the time when parishes were first formed on the Island. In 1869 Anglo-Saxon coins were discovered during the building of the bell tower. Dedicated to St Andrew, probably during the period of Scottish Rule circa 1275 to 1334, there are indications that suggest a much earlier church, whose name has been lost, occupied the site. During the Second World War the spire was removed from the church to give a clear flight path for the planes using RAF Jurby and RAF Andreas.

The Andreas carved stones are very fine examples of Dark Age craftsmanship and one, a pillar, is particularly interesting with

an inscription in Roman capitals and letters from the Ogham alphabet. Such carvings are seldom found outside Wales.

Sitting on the slopes of the Bride Hills is the village of the same name. In 1995 a new rose was named after the village. In the past things were not quite so cosy, and the village was frequently raided by pirates and marauders. On clear summer days the smoke from the Bride chimneys could be seen from the Galloway coast and the story is told that the villainous chieftain Cutlar MacCulloch and his men would, on seeing this, set sail for a good Manx feed. On one occasion arriving at a wedding feast just after soup had been taken, they devoured the meat prepared for the guests. The incident is celebrated in verse form.

The rovers were many, the wedding guests few,
So the rovers sat down to the mutton and stew,
But from that day to this, as our north custom tells,
We trust neither to wind, nor to mermaid spells,
But first of all eat - our coveted meat,
And over the broth tell of MacCulloch's feat.

To the west of Bride is Thurot Cottage, a private house whose building was made possible by utilising timbers from the defeated French Men of War lead by the "Bellisle", under the command of Captain Thurot. This battle was witnessed by Bishop Hildesley in February 1760 and would in all likelihood have been seen and certainly heard from Bride.

Bride Church and its Celtic cross are worth a visit whilst in the area, and there are a variety of pleasant walks locally.

Kirk Michael

Kirk Michael

Now using the shortened version of its name, this settlement was previously known as Kirk Michael Towne or Michaeltown. The spotlight falls on the town each year when the TT Races pass through the town - the inhabitants of Kirk Michael are said to have the flattest feet in the Isle of Man because their houses edge right up to the race course. A good place from which to watch the racing is the Mitre.

Glen Wyllin, sometimes spelt without a break between the words, meaning Mill Glen, was once a famous tourist attraction much helped by the railway. Nothing remains of the railway now except two lonely sandstone support pillars for the old bridge which used to carry the line high above the Glen. None of the beauty has been lost however, and the beach is well worth a visit.

Within the local church grounds are buried five bishops. There is a memorial stone to the popular cleric "The Good"

Bishop Wilson. He did much for the people of Ellan Vannin in his long and beneficial stewardship.

Laxey

Distances: Ballasalla 17m, Castletown 20m, Douglas 8m, Peel 19m, Port Erin 23m, Port St Mary 24m, Ramsey 8m.

Laxey translates in old Norse to 'Salmon River'. Built up over the centuries Laxey sprawls along the sides of a deep glen, running down from the mine workings in its upper reaches, to the tiny harbour at the north end of a wide bay.

Old papers of village life record that in the 18th century large shipments of fish were sent from the port to Sicily. The main products today are flour, still manufactured on the site of the 1513 mill, woollen goods and the famous Meerschaum and Briar pipes. Laxey Pipes on the Quay warmly welcome visitors to their factory shop where there are fifteen styles and six finishes to the Meerschaum to choose from.

The biggest industry Laxey ever had were the lead, copper, zinc and silver mines. Highly profitable in their heyday, between the years 1876 to 1882 the Great Laxey Mines paid out the highest total in dividends of all the lead mines in the British Isles. Earnings of this magnitude ensured a reasonable standard of living for the inhabitants.

One unmissable features of Laxey, if not the Isle of Man, is the "Lady Isabella", the biggest working water wheel in the world. Built in 1854 and named after the Governor of the day's wife, it is a stark reminder of the hard work that went into winning Laxey's wealth, pumping water from as much as two thousand feet below ground. The dimensions of the wheel are formidable with a circumference of 227 feet, and 95 steps lifting you up to the platform 75 feet from the ground.

Laxey

Manx National Heritage have done an excellent job of interpreting life as it was in the mines and the mine trail is well worth visiting.

The voluntary organisation Laxey Heritage Trust, located in the old fire station on the road just before the Wheel has a wealth of information about the village and the local area.

Lower down the glen there are gardens, the beach and a small folk museum near the station, or you can take a trip up Snaefell.

Public Amenities

Harbour Master's Office (01624) 861663

Laxey Commissioners (01624) 861241

Laxey Post Office (01624) 861209

Police Station (not continuously manned) (01624) 861210, (01624) 631212

Banks

Isle of Man Bank, New Road (01624) 637000

Tourist Information

Electric Railway Station (Seasonal) (01624) 861226

Laxey Heritage Trust, Mines Road (01624) 862007 (Restricted hours - summer only)

Lady Isabella - Laxey

Onchan

The patron saint of the Parish of Onchan was St Christopher, better known by his Gaelic name of Conchenn, meaning Dog-Head or Wolf-Head. There is a strong case to be argued that the name of the village is identified with St Connachan, who was Bishop of Sodor and Man in 540 AD.

Remarkably within the porch of St Peter's Church there are three cross slabs which depict dog-like monsters. The present church built in 1833 has no particular style of architecture, but within the churchyard there are many interesting graves amongst them being that of Lieutenant Edward Reeves RN, one of Nelson's officers who fought with him at Trafalgar.

The earlier church on this site witnessed the marriage of Captain Bligh of "Bounty" fame to a Manx girl, Elizabeth Betham, daughter of the Collector of Customs on the Island. Bligh was reputed to have rued the day that he came to the Isle of Man and met up with Fletcher Christian. The Church Register dates back to 1627 and the first vicar was appointed in 1408.

In Church Road at the place known as "The Butt" there is a quaint building with a carved head over the door. Known as Molly Caroon's cottage it was formerly used as a mission hall. Now restored it is occasionally opened to the public. Close by the cottage the Manx Nature Conservation Trust have an Urban Reserve; this wet-lands project is easily accessible and although not a large site, it is well worth a visit.

The old part of the village is grouped around the church, but with Onchan expanding so rapidly in recent years, with a number of large estates spread around the hilly countryside, the village has the second largest centre of population on the Island. A fairly new landmark is the King Edward Bay clubhouse serving a challenging and very demanding golf course laid out on the hilly terrain of Banks Howe. Near the centre of the village is Onchan Park where facilities

Douglas Bay

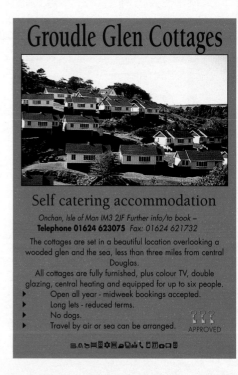

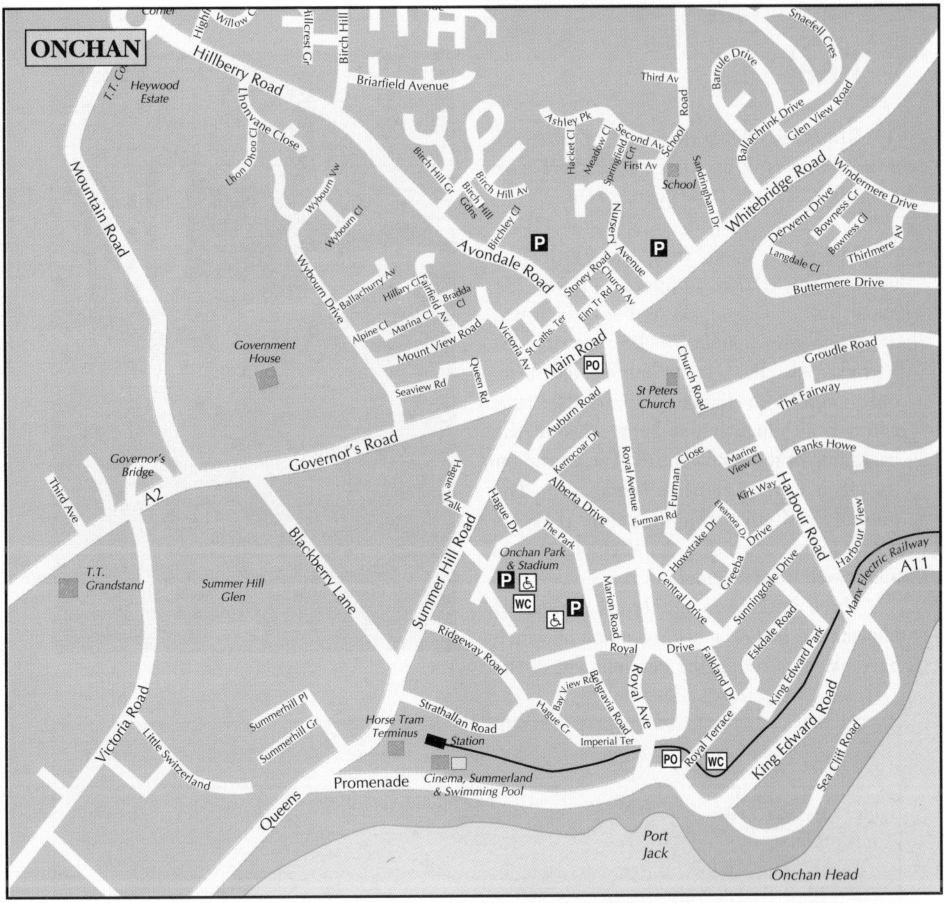

include boating, tennis, bowls, pitch and putt, and frequent stock car races.

Public Amenities

Onchan District Commissioners (Town Hall) (01624) 675564

Onchan Post Office (01624) 676031

Police Station (not continuously manned) (01624) 675190, (01624) 631212

Banks

Isle of Man Bank, Main Road (01624) 637000

Leisure Centres

Onchan Park Stadium

Horse Tram

Peel

Distances: Ballasalla 10m, Castletown 13m, Douglas 11m, Laxey 19m, Port Erin 16m, Port St Mary 16m, Ramsey 16m.

Taking its name from the castle, the name of this settlement appears in the 1231 Papal Bull of Gregory IX as Pile, which was an alternative name for Inis Patrick, St Patrick's Isle. Peel, in its abbreviated form, only came into regular use in the 19th century, although it was being used at the beginning of the 18th century. The Gaelic for the city is Purt ny Hinshey, Island Town. The present Pro-Cathedral in the centre of Peel is a fine building which gives Peel 'city' status and is well worth seeing.

There have been numerous periods of importance in Peel's history, many of which have played a roll in the development of the

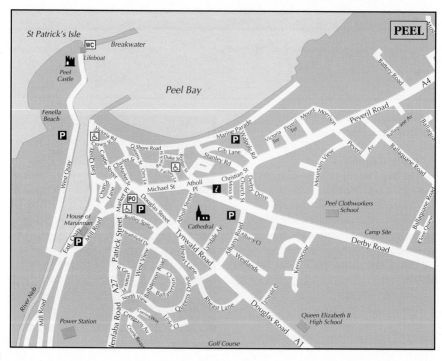

Peel

PEEL

St Patrick's Isle
WC
Breakwater
Lifeboat
Peel Castle
Peel Bay
Fenella Beach
West Quay
East Quay
Victoria Rd
Crown St
Castle Street
Shore Road
Queens St
Charles St
Market St
Beach St
Duke St
Bridge St
Factory La
Orry La
Church Lane
Michael St
Atholl Pl
Market Pl
PO
Douglas Street
Atholl Street
Cathedral
Christian St
Mona St
Church St
Derby Drive
Marine Parade
Walpole Rd
Gib Lane
Stanley Rd
Victoria Ter
Peveril Ter
Mount Morrison
Peveril Road
Battery Road
A4
Peveril Av
Ballaquane Av
Ballaquane Road
Mountain View
Peel Clothworkers School
Camp Site
Derby Road
Close Quane
House of Manannan
Mill Road
Boilley Spittal
Heathfield Dr
Patrick Street
A27
Tynwald Road
Lyndale Av
Albany Road
Albany Cl
Westlands
Kerroocoar
Rheast Lane
West View
St Germans Pl
Ballaterson Road
Ballaterson Cl
Queens Drive
North View
Tynwald C
River Neb
Mill Road
Power Station
Corrins Way
Creggans Av
Cronk Reay
Links Cl
Glenfaba Road
Douglas Road
A1
Queen Elizabeth II High School
Golf Course

Island's nation-hood. The Viking settlement of the area was one such period and excavations have uncovered important burial sites. One site revealed the remains of a female subsequently known as "The Pagan Lady". The grave was unusual in that it was a curious mixture of Christian and Pagan rituals. A very fine bead necklace was recovered from the grave which can be seen in the museum in Douglas.

Celebrated prisoners have been incarcerated in Peel Castle over the ages - William Shakespeare, makes mention in 'Henry VI' of one famous detainee, Eleanor, Duchess of Gloucester. For fourteen years the cathedral crypt was the prison of the duchess, who was accused of treason and sorcery against Henry VI as she sought to advance her husband's claim to the throne of England. Her fellow plotters were not so fortunate - Roger Bolingbroke was executed and Margery Joudemain, the Witch of Eye,

House of Manannan

was burnt to death. History records that the duchess was a difficult prisoner, who had to be carefully guarded against escape or even suicide. Her ghost is said to haunt the cathedral's crypt.

The narrow streets of Peel with their sandstone built cottages and houses act as a wonderful backdrop to the bay. The purpose of many of the buildings has changed and guessing their former use is a fascinating way of enjoying a walk around the city.

One of Peel's greatest exports has been its people and with a strong tradition of seamanship behind them many of the city's former residents spread out across the world.

You can discover much of Peel and the Island's history through to two 'Story of Mann' sites in the city – the Peel Castle Trail and the House of Manannan are part of this international award-winning tourist development.

Golf is popular and the eighteen hole course presents a fine challenge.

Public Amenities

Harbour Master's Office (01624) 842338

Peel Commissioners (Town Hall) (01624) 842341

Peel Post Office (01624) 842282

Police Station (not continuously manned) (01624) 842208, (01624) 631212

Banks

Barclays, Michael Street (Central Switchboard) (01624) 682000

Isle of Man Bank, Atholl Street (01624) 841300

Lloyds, Douglas Street (01624) 638000

Peel Castle

Port Erin

Distances Ballasalla 6m, Castletown 5m, Douglas 15m, Laxey 23m, Peel 16m, Port St Mary 2m, Ramsey 28m.

Whether you approach Port Erin by land or sea the views are impressive. Port Erin translated means either Lord's Port or Iron Port and in the Manx Gaelic it is written as Purt Chiarn. Latter day smugglers came to know Port Erin very well, using the solitude of the bay to mask their activities and kept safe from observation by the steep hills and perpendicular cliffs surrounding the village. In the last century the village became the playground of the Lancashire mill owners and their employees.

Situated at the head of an almost landlocked bay, guarded to the north by lofty Bradda Head and the Castle Rocks and Mull Peninsula to the south, Port Erin offers a sheltered play area in most weathers. Pretty

Looking towards Bradda Head

Port Erin

white painted cottages trim the inner edge of the bay, bordered by grassy banks, rising up to a more formal promenade fronting a traditional line of seaside hotels. There is a good variety of places to eat and drink.

Port Erin is a very photogenic due to the combination of sea, sand, cliffs, hill and heather. Add to that cloud shadows and brilliant sunsets often framed by Ireland's Mountains of Mourne, and you have some idea of the area's visual attraction.

Over one hundred years ago the quality of the waters offshore from Port Erin was recognised and the Marine Biological Station was established at the seaward end of the bay. Still operating, now as an annex to Liverpool University, it is well known and respected throughout the marine world. Many famous experts have consulted the station, including the late Emperor of Japan, a renowned marine life specialist, who frequently made contact - a tradition maintained by the present emperor who has visited the station in the past.

Directly opposite are the remains of a breakwater started in 1864 and meant to turn the bay into the national harbour of refuge. William Milner of Bradda Head was a staunch supporter of the breakwater and he along with everyone else on the Island would have felt a great sense of loss when in one single night in January 1884, it was destroyed in a storm.

One of the more famous residents of

Port Erin

Port Erin in recent years was former World Champion Formula 1 driver and Indianapolis Champion, Nigel Mansell, who especially enjoyed playing on the fine local golf course.

A son of Port Erin who made his way to the far side of the earth seeking fame and fortune was William Kermode, born in 1775. Taking up a grant of land in Van Diemen's Land, now of course known as Tasmania, he amassed a fortune and contributed valuable service to the Tasmanian Legislative Council. Kermode was once ambushed in his coach by two bush rangers who demanded his money or his life. Reacting faster than the robbers, he smacked their heads together, bound them up and drove to Hobart where they were arrested. His son Robert Quayle Kermode had a large say in the abolition of the Tasmania's status as a convict state.

Whilst in Port Erin it may also be worth checking with the Erin Arts Centre, which frequently holds musical and artistic events.

Port Erin

OCEAN CASTLE . PORT ERIN . ISLE OF MAN 01624 836399
FAX 01624 836537 E-MAIL: OCEANCSTLE@AOL.COM

OCEAN CASTLE HOTEL

IN THE LATE 1800'S MR JOHN CLAGUE DECIDED TO BUILD THE PORT ERIN HYDRO, AN HOTEL OF SUPERIOR ACCOMMODATION IN AN IDYLLIC SETTING

SADLY, THE HYDRO CLOSED IN 1985, LYING EMPTY AND DERELICT FOR TEN YEARS.

NOW TOTALLY RENOVATED TO IT'S FORMER GLORY, IT REOPENED IN MAY 1999.

WE HOPE WE HAVE REKINDLED THE SPIRIT OF MR CLAGUE'S VISION.

WHY NOT SEE WHAT YOU THINK?

AA
★★★

Relax, Regale & Reminisce

TOURIST BOARD
♛♛♛
COMMENDED

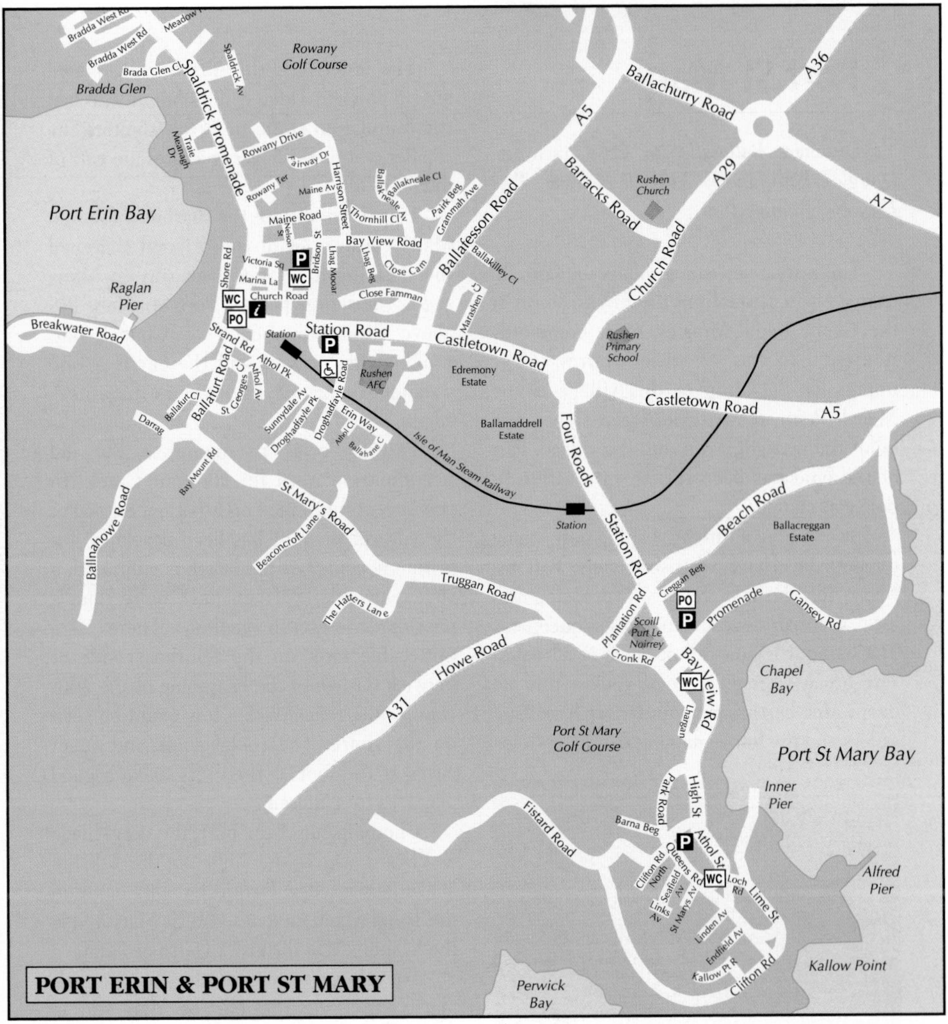

PORT ERIN & PORT ST MARY

Public Amenities

Harbour Master's Office (01624) 833205

Port Erin Commissioners Office (Town Hall) (01624) 832298

Port Erin Post Office (01624) 833119

Banks

Barclays, Station Road (Central Switchboard) (01624) 682000

Isle of Man Bank, Station Road (01624) 821400

Port St Mary

Distances: Ballasalla 7m, Castletown 4m, Douglas 16m, Laxey 24m, Peel 16m, Port Erin 2m, Ramsey 28m.

The attractive fishing village of Port St. Mary gets its name from the English form of the Gaelic Keeill Moirrey, more commonly referred to as Purt-le-Moirrey. The impressive backdrop to this village is the Meayll Peninsula with its steep slopes and fields rolling right down into the village. Part of the land has been turned into a fine 9-hole golf course.

At one time a thriving fishing port, home for both local and Scottish vessels, Port St. Mary now hosts a factory processing the local shellfish delicacy known as 'queenies'. The harbour is now full of boats of all types. The breakwater gives good shelter and its deepwater berths are popular with visiting sailors and the few remaining fishing vessels.

Port St Mary

The inner pier, the Alfred Pier, named after a previous Duke of Edinburgh who laid the foundation stone in 1882, shelters the smaller craft and is a very picturesque part of the port.

Clustered round the harbour are old Manx cottages, with the original thatched roofs having long ago given way to Manx slate. The newer part of Port St. Mary lies above the sandy beach of Chapel Bay. Linking the harbour and the bay is a fine walkway winding its way close to the water's edge.

Perwick owes its name to the old Scandinavian word for Harbour Creek. In very recent times the hotel that once stood at the edge of the cliff has been developed for private housing but the beach is still worth a visit, particularly if you have more than a passing interest in geology. There is a noticeable fault on the Southeast side of Perwick Bay. Until the beginning of the 20th century the remains of a fort could be seen on the shore. The rocky pools and small caves at the foot of the cliffs make a good play area for children.

Climbing out of the port, the next village is Fistard which sits high on the hillside above Perwick Bay. Fistard gives its name to the Treen which includes Port St Mary and is the Scandinavian for Fish's Garth or Farm.

The Howe is one of the few English place names on the Isle of Man and is derived probably from a word meaning 'of hill'.

Public Amenities

Harbour Master's Office (01624) 833206

Police Station (not continuously manned) (01624) 833222, (01624) 631212

Port St Mary Commissioners (Town Hall) (01624) 832101

Port St Mary Post Office (01624) 833113

Port St Mary

Ramsey

Distances: Ballasalla 24, Castletown 26, Douglas 16m, Laxey 8m, Peel 16m, Port Erin 28m, Port St Mary 28m.

Ramsey is situated in a beautiful setting within Ramsey Bay and with the hills of North Barrule as an impressive backdrop.

The Chronicles of Mann in about 1250 have this northern town recorded as Ramsa, seemingly drawn from the old Scandinavian language, and meaning 'Wild Garlic River'. In the Manorial Roll of 1703 the current and English spelling of the name is indicated. The Manx Gaelic has it as Ramsaa which is similar to Ramsa. Old OS maps however show the river as Stroon ny Craue, Manx for The Stream of the Wild Garlic.

There are no buildings of great antiquity in Ramsey other than Ballure Church. The Burial Register dates from 1611 and the building was reported in 1637 to be in a near ruinous state, but over the years at various times it has been restored. Bishop Wilson held a thanksgiving service here to celebrate deliverance from the French and to honour Commodore Elliot's victory. Ramsey in the last decade or so has been trying to decide whether to go for a totally modern style of rebuild or aim for a blend of the old with the new. In fact it is probably towards the latter they are drifting and there is a happy mingling of architectural styles, particularly on the sea front.

Presumably the reason for much of Ramsey's lack of old buildings lies in the fact that it was the site of much destruction across the centuries. Olaf, King of Mann, was murdered by his nephew Reginald near the harbour in 1154. Somerled, the twelfth century Thane of Argyll, made a historic landing here, and Robert the Bruce a century later passed through on his way to besiege Castle Rushen.

Ramsey harbour

Landing in Ramsey became a lot easier when the magnificent Ramsey Pier was built. Thrusting itself out into deep water it quickly became a popular stopping off point for the steamers en route to other ports of call, and today it is a working harbours that offers berths to yachts, coasters and trawlers. The harbour is the HQ of the Manx Sailing and Cruising Club, which as well as organising smaller local races is also responsible for the prestigious Isle of Man Round the Island Yacht Race every summer.

An unmissable feature of the harbour is the 225' long iron swing bridge, opened in 1892. The Ramsey Ship Yard, beyond the swing bridge, constructed one of the world's first iron ships as well as the 'Star of India', a famous attraction in the American port city of San Diego. Ramsey's shipyard also built the world's first two ships specifically designed as oil tankers.

Situated at the mouth of the Island's

Looking towards the Scottish coast

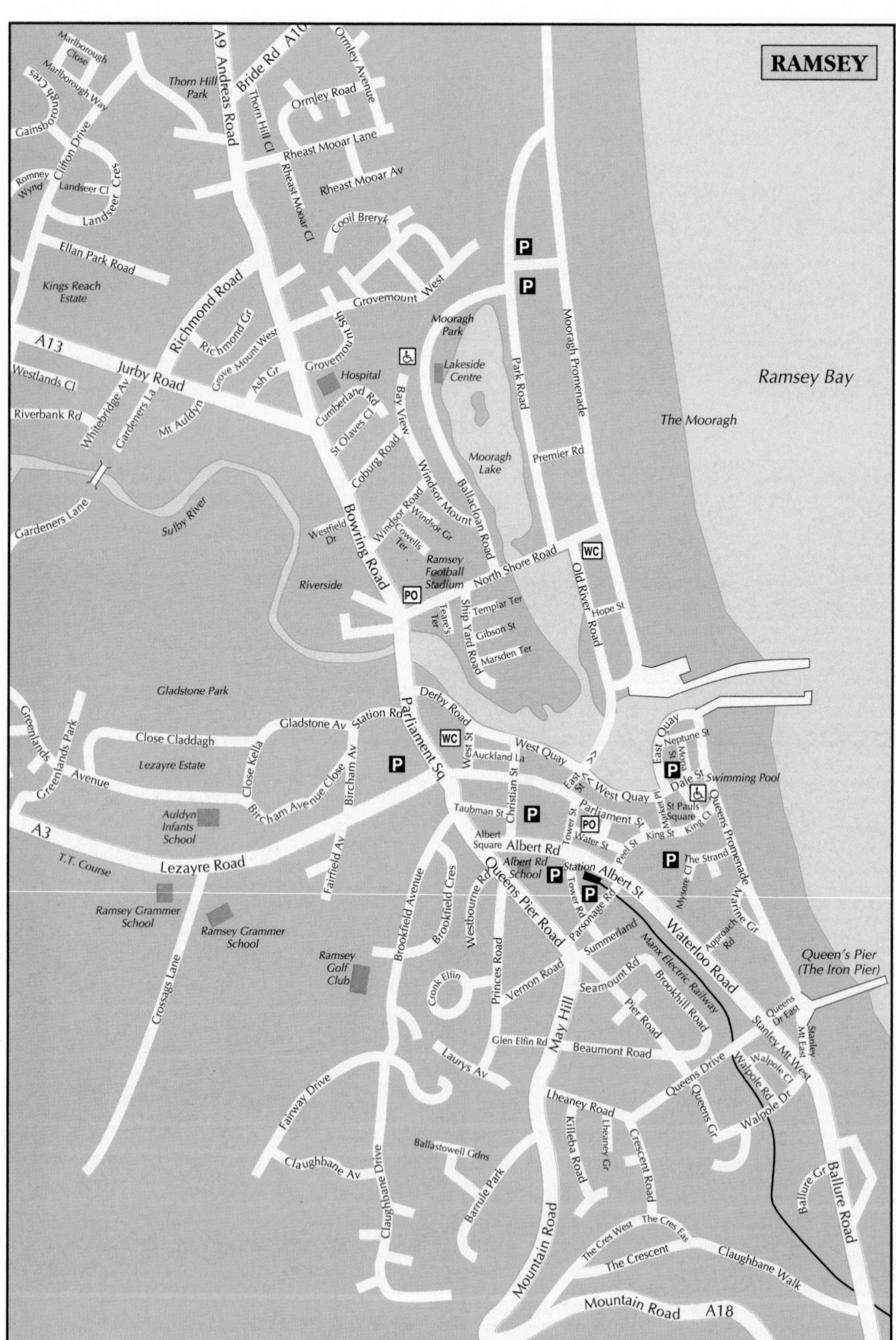
RAMSEY
Ramsey Bay
The Mooragh
Marlborough Close
Marlborough Way
Gainsborough Cres
Clifton Drive
Romney Wynd
Landseer Cl
Landseer Cres
Ellan Park Road
Kings Reach Estate
Thorn Hill Park
A9 Andreas Road
Bride Rd A10
Thorn Hill Cl
Ormley Avenue
Ormley Road
Rheast Mooar Lane
Rheast Mooar Cl
Rheast Mooar Av
Cooil Breryk
Grovemount West
Grovemount Sth
Richmond Road
Richmond Gr
Grove Mount West
Ash Gr
A13
Jurby Road
Westlands Cl
Riverbank Rd
Whitebridge Av
Gardeners La
Mt Auldyn
Gardeners Lane
Sulby River
Mooragh Park
Lakeside Centre
Hospital
Cumberland Rd
St Olaves Cl
Bay View
Coburg Road
Windsor Road
Windsor Mount
Windsor Gr
Cowells Ter
Westfield Dr
Bowring Road
Ballacloan Road
Mooragh Lake
Park Road
Mooragh Promenade
Premier Rd
Ramsey Football Stadium
North Shore Road
Riverside
PO
WC
Old River Road
Hope St
Teare's Ter
Ship Yard Road
Templar Ter
Gibson St
Marsden Ter
Gladstone Park
Derby Road
Parliament Sq
Station Rd
Gladstone Av
Close Claddagh
Lezayre Estate
Close Kella
Greenlands
Greenlands Park
Avenue
Bircham Av
Bircham Avenue Close
West St
Auckland La
West Quay
Christian St
East St
East Quay
Neptune St
Mona St
Dale St
Swimming Pool
Market Pl
St Pauls Square
King Ct
Queens Promenade
Parliament St
Taubman St
Tower St
Water St
Peel St
King St
Albert Square
Albert Rd
Albert Rd School
Station
Albert St
The Strand
Mysore Cl
Auldyn Infants School
A3
T.T. Course
Lezayre Road
Fairfield Av
Brookfield Avenue
Brookfield Cres
Westbourne Rd
Queens Pier Road
Tower Rd
Parsonage Rd
Waterloo Road
Marine Gr
Approach Rd
Ramsey Grammer School
Ramsey Grammer School
Crossags Lane
Ramsey Golf Club
Summerland
Manx Electric Railway
Brookhill Road
Seamount Rd
Princes Road
Vernon Road
Cronk Elfin
May Hill
Pier Road
Queen's Pier (The Iron Pier)
Queens Dr East
Stanley Mt East
Stanley Mt West
Glen Elfin Rd
Beaumont Road
Laurys Av
Walpole Cl
Walpole Rd
Queens Drive
Queens Gr
Walpole Dr
Fairway Drive
Lheaney Road
Killeba Road
Lheaney Gr
Crescent Road
Ballastowell Gdns
Claughbane Av
Claughbane Drive
Barrule Park
Ballure Gr
Ballure Road
Mountain Road
The Cres West
The Cres Eas
The Crescent
Claughbane Walk
Mountain Road A18

longest river, the Sulby, Ramsey was once an island. In 1630 the town was virtually destroyed by the sea, a continuous threat until the early years of the 19th century. Mooragh Park was created in 1881 after the re-direction of the river and the silting up of the old harbour entrance. This comprises 40 acres of gardens with a 12 acre boating lake as the centre piece. Concerts and galas are held in the park in summer and at the Lakeside Centre.

There are several festivals in Ramsey each year, including Yn Chruinnaght, a week long festival of music, dance, art and literature from the six Celtic nations of Mann, Cornwall, Scotland, Ireland, Wales and Brittany, later in the year the park also hosts several vintage motor rallies during the TT and the Manx Grand Prix and Ramsey Carnival Day in July.

The town also had a number of fine museums, including the Manx Electric Railway Museum, the Gibbs of the Grove Museum and the Ballagunnell Farm Museum at nearby Andreas.

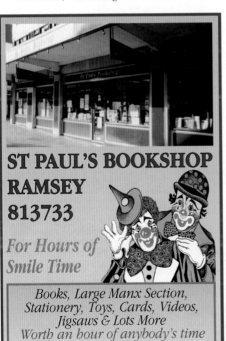

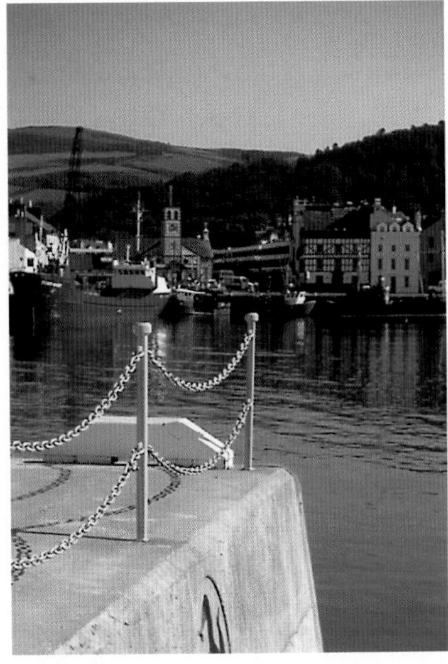

Ramsey harbour

Golfers should try a round or two at the challenging Ramsey Golf Club; walkers can put in plenty of miles along the nearby coasts and hills; and if you want to get rid of your money try the shopping along Parliament Street, St. Paul's Square, the Victoria Mall and the quayside. There is also a market every Saturday in summer at the Market Square.

Moving in or out of Ramsey is easy by public transport, but please note the electric trams operate a reduced service during the winter.

Public Amenities

Harbour Master's Office (01624) 812245

Police Station (01624) 812234

Ramsey Cottage Hospital (01624) 811811

Ramsey Town Commissioners (Town Hall) (01624) 812228

Ramsey Post Office, Court Row (01624) 812248

Banks

Barclays, Parliament Street (01624) 684444

Isle of Man Bank, Parliament Street (01624) 811200

Lloyds TSB, Parliament Street (01624) 683200

HSBC, St Paul's Square (01624) 684851

TSB Bank, Parliament Street (01624) 813596

Building Societies

Britannia (IOM), Parliament Street (01624) 681190

Leisure Centres

The Venture Centre (01624) 814240

Mooragh Park (01624) 813375

Ramsey Swimming Pool, Queens Promenade (01624) 812852

St John's

Inland and to the East of Peel is St John's. Dotted about the guide are various references to the politically important role that this attractive village has played and continues to play in the life of the Isle of Man. Sitting comfortably with an air of elegance, hugging the gap between Slieau Whallian and Beary Mountain - traced back to the Scandinavian for Farm of the Shieling - it is well worth a visit.

Every 5th July, the Isle of Man's National Day, the Island celebrates over a thousand years of unbroken government by holding the traditional open air Tynwald at St. John's. Thousand of people make the journey to watch the ancient ceremony. The laws of Mann which have been enacted during the last year are proclaimed in Manx and English, in summarised form, by the Deemsters - the Manx equivalent of British High Court Judges - to the gathered public,

St John's

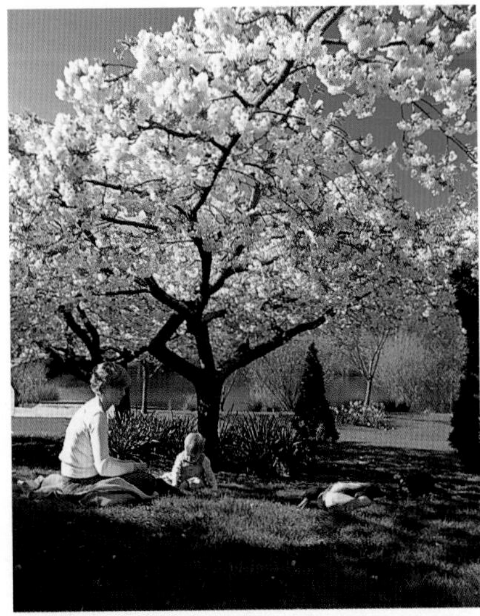

Spring blossom at St John's

after which Tynwald has a formal meeting within the Royal Chapel of St John's.

Sitting on the summit of Tynwald Hill is the Lieutenant Governor. Below him and arranged in descending order are variously the Keys, Legislative Council, Crown Officers, Churchmen, Heads of Local Authorities, Captains of the Parishes and the six Coroners of the Island. A fair supports the formal part of the day.

One of the most popular developments of recent years has seen the site of the old Tynwald Woollen Mills changed from the production of fine woollen garments into a full blown craft and shopping centre. There is plenty of parking at the complex and it is on the bus routes and coach tour itineraries. There are play areas for children, and excellent catering facilities.

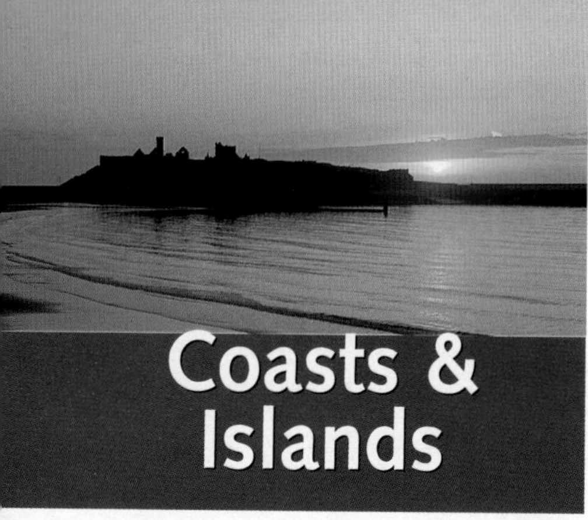

Coasts & Islands

The coastline of the Isle of Man is varied and fascinating. The Island being so small, it is inevitable that you will end up back at the coast again and again. This is a good thing.

Historically, the sea has played an important role in the story of the Isle of Man, so it is no surprise that much of what goes on here happens on the coast, even today. Legacies and reminders of previous generations of inhabitants are prevalent and the scenery is often spectacular, in places as breathtaking as any coastline you will see anywhere in the British Isles

The approximately 100 miles of coastline may be roughly divided into two. From Maughold to Peel, round the south of the Island, is maritime hardcliff. These rocky cliffs include some of the remotest places on the Island, least affected by human activity, and provide great breeding grounds for numerous bird species. The vegetation along the footpaths is also very interesting. The other half of the coast, from Glen Mooar to Ramsey round the north end, is predominantly sand and shingle, or maritime soft cliff and dune. This section includes the Ayres, an area of particular ecological interest that has been registered as an Area of Special Scientific Interest (ASSI). Again, the plant life and birds are of interest.

Though there is only really one satellite island, there are a number of small islets that are of significance either historically or ecologically.

For this chapter, the coast has been broken up into a few sections, starting in Ramsey and running clockwise around the Island.

The Coast

Ramsey to Douglas

South of Ramsey, the coastline becomes rugged again approaching Maughold Head. The water here is a luxurious blue colour. The white lighthouse on the headland looks fine, hanging above the sea. Half a mile back along the Maughold Brooghs, the view, on a good day, is superb. Out to sea, you can see Burrow Head in Scotland, the Cumbrian Hills and Snowdonia (as well as Sellafield).

Laxey is tucked up the mouth of the Great Glen and protected by the twin headlands of Laxey head and Clay Head.

Douglas to Spanish Head

The tall cliffs at Douglas Head diminish incrementally all the way down to Derbyhaven. A road, rather romantically named 'Marine Drive', follows the coast for a few miles from Douglas as far as Port Soderick. Thereafter, if you are on foot and following the Raad Ny Foillan, the cliff tops are beautiful all the way to the airport, near Derbyhaven. Seagulls and fulmars have colonies all along the rocky cliffs.

On a low promontory above Port Grenaugh, there is a Celtic fort called Cronk ny Merriu (which means 'House of the Dead'). The Vikings subsequently used the fort and there are remains of a rectangular Viking house within the original fortifications.

On Langness and around Derbyhaven, there are large populations of wading birds including curlew, ringed plover and oystercatchers. Langness is also well known for its lovely wildflowers.

Near Spanish Head, there is a area of land owned by the Manx National Trust

Marine Drive

called the Chasms, which you can reach from the car park at the bottom of the lane from Cregneash. There are huge fissures here, some 100 feet deep, covered over by gorse and heather. Great care should be taken walking here, especially if you are with children. Stay on the footpath. When you get close to the coast, look out for the Sugar Loaf, a lonely conical rock 100 feet tall, coming out of the Irish Sea. This rock has abundant ledges favoured by guillemot, razorbill and kittiwake for breeding.

Spanish Head is so called because a galleon from the Spanish Armada is reputed to have been wrecked here. This is a great picnic spot and if you look carefully, you may well see seals bobbing about in the turbulent water. Shags like nesting here, using sticks and seaweed to make nests on the cliffs.

The Isle of Man lies ' in the arms' of a prevailing south-west wind which has driven strong seas up from St George's channel and done much to shape this end of the Island. In the winter months, if you can fight you way down to Spanish Head in a gale, the sight of the ocean combers hurling themselves at the cliffs here and on the calf is impressive.

Spanish Head

The Sound to Glen Mooar

The rugged cliffs continue round the southern point of the Island and up the west coast. Along the edge of Bay Fine look out for basking sharks. Apparently it helps to wear sunglasses when trying to spot them.

Milner's Tower on top of Bradda Head, the promontory north of Port Erin, was built in 1871 to commemorate the connection between Port Erin and William Milner, the famous Liverpudlian manufacturer of safes who lived in Port Erin. There used to be a permanent coastguard post here, but now it is used only in big storms.

The coastal footpath along the Bradda Hills is a delight. The cliff edge here falls sheer into the sea. On a decent day, you can see Slieve Donard in Ireland and the outline of the mountains of Mourne. Cronk ny Arrey Laa is the crown of this long stretch of cliffs at 427 metres (1,400 feet). These magnificent cliffs were shot for the opening sequence of the feature film 'Waking Ned'.

Below Cronk ny Arrey Laa, only 100 metres above the sea on the most exposed coast of the Island is an early Christian 'keill' or chapel. Nearly 200 'keill' sites have been discovered on the Island, but few are more austere in their location than this one. It is thought to date from the middle of the 5th Century. Their architectural form is very simple and the remains are not exactly thrilling, but if you fancy visiting only one 'keill', see this one.

The rocky coast also provides a nesting habitat for some non-seabird species including the raven, chough and the peregrine falcon. The Isle of Man has an internationally important number of breeding chough and peregrine numbers are thought to be at an all time high.

Above Peel, on top of Corrin's Hill, is Corrin's Folly. Nearby is St Patrick's Well, a

Calf of Man

spot revered by early Christians. Legend has it that when St Patrick landed here, the horse he was riding shed a silver shoe. Spring water immediately sprung forth, forming the well.

All along this fine stretch of coast, you can find plants that manage to grow amongst the rocks. These include lichens, thrift, sea campion, rock samphire and red fescue. In the grassland areas, you will also find birdsfoot trefoil and the beautiful blue spring squill.

Glen Mooar to Ramsey

The section of coast, round the north of the Island is not as dramatic as the rocky extremities in the south, but it is perhaps more interesting for ecological reasons.

The Ayres derives its name from the old Norse word eyrr meaning 'gravelbank'. The soft cliff and dune here is still changing as the hills to the south are being eroded and some of this material is being deposited.

Marram grass (used locally as thatching and known as bent) stabilises the dunes and plants colonising the dunes include sea holly, sea bindweed, sea spurges, the Isle of Man cabbage and the pyramidal orchid.

Just inland, heath has developed on the thin soil and heathers, western gorse and other grasses grow here. The Ayres are notable for small breeding colonies of Arctic and little terns (rare British seabirds), along with mallard, shelduck, lapwings, curlew and oystercatchers. You are also likely to see gannets, shags and cormorants diving for fish.

There is a visitor centre and nature trail at the Ayres, run by the Manx National Conservation Trust. Please take care when visiting the Ayres. The ecology is fragile.

Islands

The Calf of Man

The Calf of Man is a bird sanctuary and observatory maintained by Manx National Heritage. There is a resident warden and

Peel harbour

many birds are ringed during migration periods. Many seabirds breed here and there is a large population of chough. The cliffs and springy turf are nesting grounds for a huge variety of birds.

It has, in fact, been famous for its seabirds for over three hundred years and particularly for its colony of Manx Shearwater. They were harvested for food and oil, which was used in the treatment of wool and for cleaning firearms. The population was decimated in the 18th century when, it is thought, rats escaped to the Calf from a ship.

It is possible to visit the Calf during the summer months. Regular sailings operate from Port Erin harbour. If you happen to be in your own boat, take instruction about where to land and great care in doing so. You can stay overnight in the spartan accommodation provided at the Observatory, by prior arrangement through Manx National Heritage.

The Calf has a circumference of eight kilometres (five miles) and a land mass of 616 acres. It takes about half a day to explore all of it. Its history is discursive, probably because of the problems reaching it. A Celtic stone cross, a cross said to unique in the world, depicting the crucifixion, was discovered there can now be seen in the Manx Museum.

The Chicken Rock

This is a small islet off the Calf. There is a reef here, on the edge of a steep descent deep into the Irish Sea. The lighthouse was built in 1875, to replace the earlier lighthouses on the Calf. It is now fully automated.

St Patrick's Isle

"No part of the Isle of Man has played so great and interesting a part in the history as the islet known as Peel Island, or St Patrick's Isle" – Canon Stenning. In any history or modern photographic portrait of the Island, the name recurs constantly. The first mention of the islet occurs in the 'Annals of Ulster' for the years 797-8 AD. Numerous periods of architecture from prehistoric earthworks to Napoleonic fortifications are represented. It has been a garrison, an armoury, and an ecclesiastical prison. Eight bishops are believed to be have been buried here. The remains of the fortifications and St Germain's Cathedral are wonderful and no trip to the Isle of Man is complete without visiting it.

Conister Rock

If you reach the Island by ship, arriving in Douglas, you cannot miss this romantic rock in the middle of the bay. The Tower of Refuge on it was built by Sir William and Lady Hillary in 1832 as a refuge to shelter the shipwrecked sailors from vessels that had been driven by gales and storms onto these jagged and dangerous rocks. Sir William went on to found the Royal National Lifeboat Institution - the RNLI.

St Michael's Isle

A short causeway joins this islet to Langness. There are the remains of a 17th Century stone round fort built for The Seventh Earl of Derby, Yn Stanlagh Mooar, who clearly feared for his kingdom. Remains of earth embankments are still clearly visible on the Island and it is thought that they may have been raised at the time of Magnus's landing here in 1250. There is also a ruined chapel, which probably stands on the site of an ancient 'keill' and a close inspection of the building reveals alterations to its dimensions at different times.

There is a story about the priest who proposed that a new church should be built on St Michael's Isle. The idea for the twelfth or early thirteenth century church had come to him in a vision during which St Michael pointed out the location of the building and a finely designed altar within. Working with a will the people gave their labour freely and

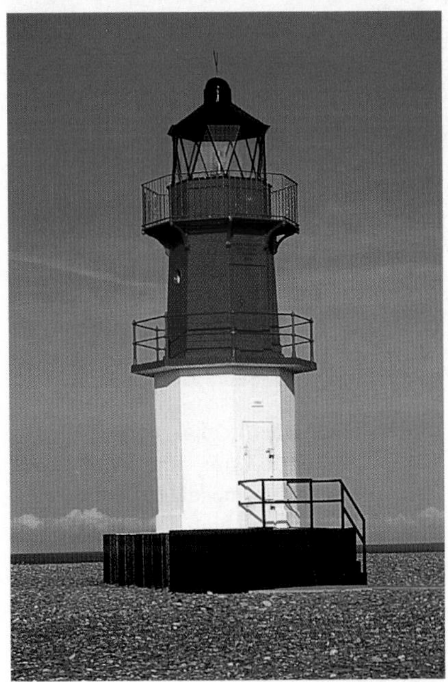

Point of Ayre

finished the church. There was however no way they could provide the fine altar seen in the vision. Then, the confession of a dying shipwrecked pirate revealed a horde of gold buried in the churchyard. When convinced that there was no one left alive to whom the treasure could belong, this priest bought a statue of the Madonna and around the neck hung a string of pearls found with the treasure. Later, a ship anchored in Derbyhaven and two of the crew came ashore, begging the priest to come out to their vessel and minister to one of their colleagues. Suspecting nothing, he went with them. But it was another pirate ship and they knew about the treasure. The next morning the villagers found the church had been sacked and their priest murdered by the very pearls from around the statue's neck. To this very day it is believed that whoever strikes the walls of this ancient building will hear the moans of the saintly victim, accompanied by the jingle of coins.

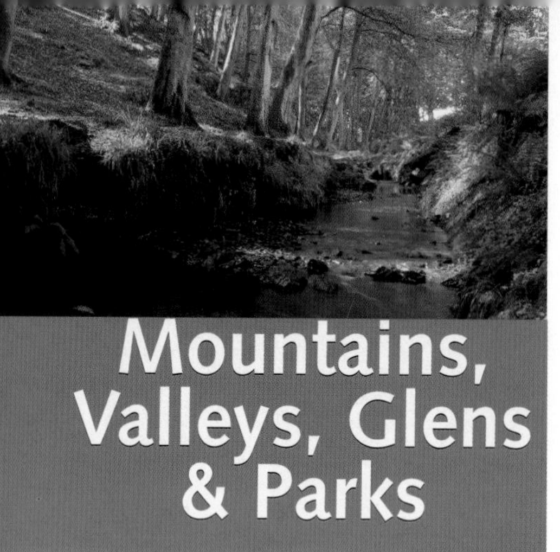

Mountains, Valleys, Glens & Parks

To appreciate the topography of the Isle of Man, its size and its dramatic position in the middle of the Irish Sea, you really have to climb to the top of it. Snaefell is the highest peak. At 621 metres (2,036 feet) it is no giant, but the view, on a clear day, will take your breath away (if, of course, you have any left after the walk). Naturally, you can see most of the Island itself. Beyond the sea, looking to the east are the Cumbrian Mountains, to the north, the purple headed hills of Galloway, in the west the Mountains of Mourne in Ulster and further south the Wicklow Mountains, and finally looking directly south you can see Snowdonia in north Wales.

Forty per cent of the Island's landmass is uninhabited. Again, this is only really appreciated from on high. The range of hills runs on a Northeast to Southwest axis, from Ramsey to Cronk ny Arrey Laa (thought to mean 'hill of the day watch'), north of Port Erin, where the cliffs drop steeply into the sea. Though there is a central valley running from Peel to Douglas, splitting the northern and southern uplands, the range can be regarded as one large slate massif. Snaefell is situated comfortably in the middle of the range, and there are 25 finely sculpted peaks over 1,000 feet fitting snugly around it. This means that you can stride across the uplands, through the gorse and heather, for a day, peering over the east and west coasts, without having to descend and ascend too much.

The hills afford some of the wildest places on the Island with spectacular scenery, particularly in late summer when they are clad in purple heather. This heath provides a rare habitat for diverse wildlife and is of international importance. Ling, western gorse, bell heather, and bilberry are the dominant plants. Blanket bog is another globally rare habitat found in the uplands.

Birdlife is good up here and includes curlews, skylarks, meadow pipits and wheatear. The Isle of Man has perhaps 10% of the British hen harrier population and there are good populations of peregrine and raven.

The hills have broad ridges with relatively smooth slopes, which merge into wide drainage basins. Streams cutting into the hillsides have produced the glens that the Isle of Man is famous for.

Large areas of the uplands were once covered in forest. The loss of the trees in neolithic times probably resulted in waterlogging and the peat formation, which the Manx people relied on for fuel until relatively recently. In Viking times, many people lived on the uplands in summer, grazing livestock on the common pasture and the remains of the settlements, called 'sheilings' can still be seen.

Glens

Though there are few valleys of significance, the Isle of Man is famous for its glens. There are 17 glens, all owned by the Manx government. They may be roughly divided into mountain glens and coastal glens. They vary in physical length, breadth and isolation but they are all beautiful in their own way.

The rushing waters of the steep glens were once put to good use for milling, mineral extraction and to drive turbines in the manufacture of paper amongst other

Manx countryside in spring

industrial uses. You will find disused mines shafts and buildings in many of the glens. During the Victorian era, when many tourists visited the Island, pleasure gardens were created. Now, the largest areas of established broad-leafed woodlands are the Manx National Glens.

For a more thorough information sheet on the glens, ask in a TIC. The following is a brief introduction to a few of them.

Mountain Glens

Sulby Glen, also known as Tholt-e-Will Glen starts from a spring in peat-moss on the west slopes of Snaefell and runs down to Sulby. It is river-worn, deep and bold and gives you an image of the grandest of Manx scenery in miniature. The Sulby River is the longest and largest river in the Island.

Glen Auldyn is perhaps the gentlest of Manx mountain glens and starts on the north of Snaefell as a trickling rill, then runs down through forest and a couple of hamlets to Milntown on the B17. The views at the top end are grand.

Coastal Glens

One of the loveliest of the short glens is Ballaglass Glen. You can walk its length from near the top of Clagh Ouyr, or just a section of it nearer the sea. The wooded section further down is wonderful in spring when the bluebells is out. The area is rich with folklore and here you might just encounter the spectre of the giant Irish deer, the 'Londhoo'.

Dhoon Glen, a little further south along the coast from Cornaa, is typical of the quaint coastal glens. There is a car park by the tram stop on the A2. From there the walk down to the beach will take half an hour.

Parks

At the time of the Victorian tourist boom in the Isle of Man, a great number of parks were developed. Though many have lost their grandeur, they can still be very pleasant

QUALITY MEATS FROM THE ISLE OF MAN

QUALITY THAT STANDS · THE TEST OF TIME ·

FARM SOURCED, FARM ASSURED
TRADITIONAL MEAT
FROM
THE ISLE OF MAN

Sulby Glen

places to while away an afternoon. Most are owned and run by the government and access is free. There are a few private parks and gardens on the Island which are usually only open to the public for fund raising events or special occasions. One exception however is the dramatic Ballalheannagh Gardens in Glen Roy, which is open all year.

St John's

The Arboretum at St John's is a fine spot for a picnic. The park is full of trees and bushes, gifted to the Manx nation by world governments in celebration of the Tynwald Millennium, the thousandth year of the Manx Parliament. If in St John's, visit the Department's of Agriculture's nursery gardens.

Douglas

Douglas has many parks and gardens and excellent gardeners who look after them. Pride of place has to be given to the "Sunken Gardens" on Douglas Promenade. Each year the gardens are virtually redesigned and special themes are used to celebrate anniversaries and other special dates. Noble's Park along with the Villa Marina and its gardens was donated to the town by Henry Bloom Noble, and are renowned for their sporting facilities, offering bowls, tennis and many other leisure uses. At night, from July to October, children may enjoy walking down through Summer Hill Glen where there are fairy lights and illuminated animal displays. Douglas celebrated its centenary as a borough in 1996 and one of the ways it recognised this landmark was with a yellow florabunda rose. Named as "Douglas Centenary" it was available by mail order and you can see a bed of them in the Villa Marina Gardens.

Onchan

To the north end of Douglas Bay is Onchan Park, which has entertainment for all the family and within walking distance of most of the Douglas hotels.

Laxey

Laxey has fine natural gardens. The site of the old mine washing floors has been turned into a garden to blend in with the surrounding landscape and offers good shelter on blustery days. The village is also close to the famous Ballalheannagh Gardens at Glen Roy. Tucked away in one of the most beautiful glens in the Island. These gardens are off the beaten track but easily accessible by car, taxi or mini-bus. To find the gardens follow the B12 from Creg-ny-Baa towards Laxey and turn left just before Social Cottage. If you approach from Laxey take the Glen Roy Road which goes up the hill from the petrol station. The gardens are built into steep hillsides and cleverly use every inch of the terrain with waterfalls and cascades. Four miles of gravel paths lead to displays of Ericaceae, Rhododendron, Eucryphia, Pieris, Betula, Alnus and Sorbus. There are over 10,000 different plants. The gardens are open daily from 10am to 1pm and from 2pm to 5pm. There is an admission charge. Call 861875 for further information.

Watching the waters rush by

Ramsey

The biggest park in Ramsey is the Mooragh. There are rowing boats, canoes, pedaloes and sailing dinghies for hire or you can learn to sail, canoe or windsurf. They are also a bowling green, crazy golf and a putting green. The Town Commissioners in conjunction with the local Rotarians have developed wasteland along the banks of the Sulby River as a natural park. Known as Poyll Dooey, it translates as Pool of the Black Ford and a walk through the area brings you to a ford which was the main crossing point between north and south Ramsey long before the town's bridges were built.

The Curraghs

Near Ballaugh, on the A3, is the Wildlife Park. It is set in natural surroundings and visitors can wander through the enclosures, observing the animals and birds at close quarters. New arrivals include a pair of Indian fishing cats and a lynx. There is a walk through Aviary and an Ark, which explains some environmental issues. There is a cafe by a small lake. Guardians of the lake are undoubtedly the spider monkeys, just watch them control the waterfront. Besides looking for the new animals and birds, ask for a copy of the Park's new Guide Book, it's full of fascinating information. Children love the Wildlife Park with its nature trails and there are play areas designed to let them work off their surplus energy. During the summer the miniature railway "The Orchid Line" provides further diversion.

Mountains, Valleys, Glens
& Parks

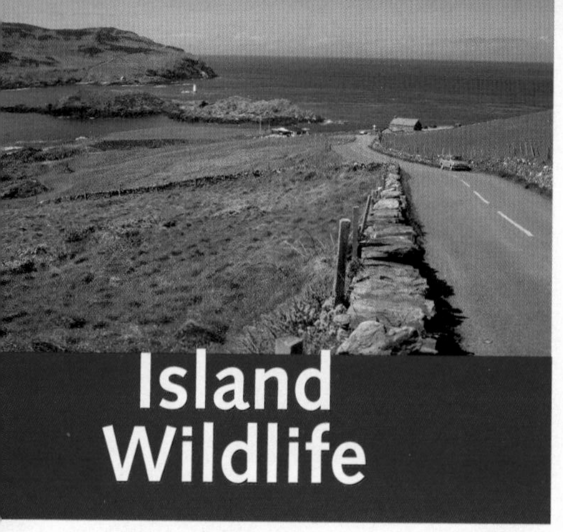

Island Wildlife

The Isle of Man's position in the middle of the Irish Sea has given it a unique ecology. For example, there are no snakes here (as in Ireland) and no badgers, newts, woodpeckers or several other species native to many parts of the British Isles.

Birdlife

The Island has a rich assortment of bird species, including some relatively rare species such as the chough, peregrine falcon and hen harrier. This is largely due to the wide variety of habitats. The Calf of Man has an important bird observatory, administered by Manx National Heritage.

Raven, fulmar and shag are quite common along the coastline, and the steeper cliffs of the Island have colonies of guillemots, black guillemot and kittiwakes. However, cormorants are limited – the only colonies are at Maughold, Ladyport, Will's Strand, Pistol Castle and Baie Fine.

One of the most outstanding wildlife success stories on the Isle of Man has been that of the hen harrier. The harriers first nested in 1977 in Glen Rushen, since when more than 40 pairs have nested on the Island, and Ballaugh Curraghs has the largest roost in Western Europe, as well as having plenty of variety of other bird life year-round.

The gorse and bramble scrub that is common on many coastal slopes is important for stonechats (the name comes from the sound they make, like two pebbles being knocked together), and on rocky coastlines you may come across purple sandpipers, whilst the ground-nesting little tern is the most important breeding bird on the Ayres shore.

Inland the fast flowing streams and wooded glens provide a habitat for grey wagtails, chiffchaff, blackcap and treecreeper – look out for them at Ballaglass, Tholt-y-Will, Glen Helen or Glen Maye. On the wooded slopes of the Island's northern plain sparrowhawks and woodcock can be seen, whilst forestry areas may harbour siskin and crossbill, and in smaller plantations long-eared and short-eared owls may be seen (long-eared are the commonest). The numerous reservoirs on the Island are an important habitat for wildfowl such as pochard and tufted duck.

This is only the briefest of summaries of the Isle of Man's bird life, and if you wish to know more call in at a TIC where you can pick up a leaflet describing the best 'birding' sites and details of guidebooks to the Island's birds.

Wildflowers

Wildflower habitats are important, especially the shingle beach at the Ayres and the Manx Wildlife Trust's reserve at Close Sartfield, Ballaugh Curraghs. Here there are over 100,000 orchids, varying in colour from deep purple to pale pink and providing a carpet of colour in the spring and summer. You may see pale pink heath-spotted orchids, pinky-purple common orchids, O'Kelly's spotted orchid, dark salmon-pink early marsh orchids, bright purple northern marsh orchids, butterfly orchids and Britain's most common orchid, the common twayblade.

Early summer is also the time to see the distinctive wildflowers of the coastal slopes, woodland glades and hedgerows. Sea pinks, spring squill, bluebells, Isle of Man cabbage, sea bindweed and sea holly are just a few of the many brightly coloured species that bring the landscape alive with colour in the warmer months.

Grey Seals

One of the most important Manx wildlife sanctuaries on the Island is the Calf of Man - a beautiful islet of just 616 acres, accessible to summer visitors by boat from Port Erin. Between 1962 and 1990, almost 100,000 birds of 134 species were ringed at the bird observatory here. The bird population shares the islet with a flock of Manx Loaghtan sheep (Loaghtan is Manx for mouse brown). These multi-horned sheep are the only surviving truly Manx breed of farm animal.

There are many other places around the Island where wildlife can be observed in its natural habitat. Atlantic grey seals are year-round residents, with breeding colonies at Maughold Head and the Calf of Man. If you're visiting the Calf, the boatman may well take a detour to show you the seals. From late August onwards you may see several generations of grey seals in the water or 'hauled out' in the sun, from white-furredpups through to light grey 'yearlings' and the darker and bigger male and female adults – the bulls especially can be an impressive sight.

Manx countryside in summer

Basking shark

Basking Sharks

The basking shark that is the real offshore star of the Manx wildlife scene. The Isle of Man is one of the best places in the world to see this, the world's second largest fish. Existing entirely on plankton, these huge but harmless creatures can grow up to ten metres in length and weigh as much as five tonnes – they feed by filtering plankton out of the sea water, and in one hour a basking shark may take in enough water to fill a 50-metre swimming pool.

The Isle of Man Basking Shark Society runs shark-sighting trips from south from Peel past Fleshwick Bay and Niarbyl most weekends between June and September.

According to director Ken Watterson, everyone should see at least one shark, and you may also see grey seals, dolphins and orca and minke whales.

The sharks migrate up the Irish Sea, passing the Island between June and September (although they have been seen as early as January) before heading north past the west coast of Scotland and leaving British waters in October. Ken Watterson says shark numbers have declined in recent years, but he is confident this has been turned around and that numbers will increase to former levels in the future.

Other wildlife attractions include the Ayres Visitor Centre, the Marine Interpretation Centre at Port Erin, the Scarlett Visitor Centre in Castletown and several other nature reserves and areas of wetlands managed by the Manx Nature Conservation Trust. For more information on Island wildlife contact the Island's TIC.

***Wildlife Calendar** – a brief guide to just some of the wildlife activity you may see on the Isle of Man throughout the year.*

January

Wintersweet in flower. Whooper swans in Jurby parish. Golden plover over-wintering on the Ayres.

February

Lesser celandine in flower in sheltered spots. Song and mistle thrushes in song. Rooks and ravens becoming active.

March

Primroses in flower and first of the year's butterflies can be seen.

April

Marsh marigolds in full bloom. Wood anemones flowering in the glens. Willow warblers arriving to breed. Ferns beginning to unfold.

May

Sea pink and bluebells in bloom. Swallows and martins in full flight.

June

Orchids in full bloom. Yellow flag iris in flower. The roding (soft croaking call) of the male woodcock can be heard in the evenings at Ballaugh Curraghs.

July

Manx hay meadows at their most colourful. Seabird concentrations off the Ayres coast. Basking sharks frequently seen.

August

Abundance of red admiral and painted lady butterflies. Wetland plants in flower. Skuas busy chasing terns.

September

Hills take on purple and yellow hue. Fuchsias shedding their blooms. Red-throated divers appear in good numbers in the north.

October

Influx of winter thrushes, redwings and fieldfare. Autumn colours in glens. Seals can be heard singing.

November

Hen harriers roosting at Close Sartfield Nature Reserve. Ducks in full breeding plumage.

December

Carpets of mosses and liverworts found in northern glens. Mountain hares wearing winter coats.

Island Wildlife

Wild Flowers at the coast in the spring

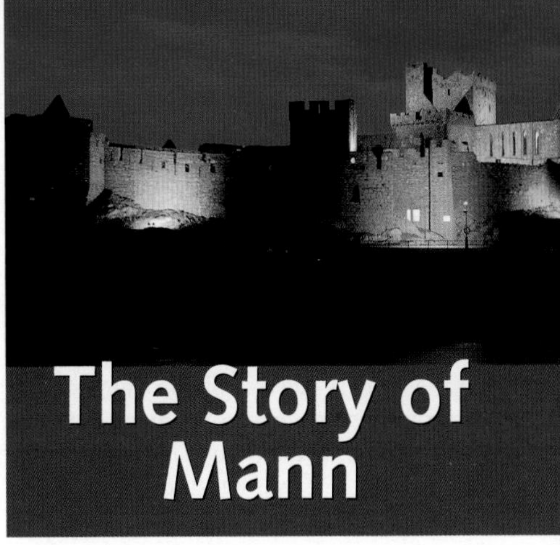

The Story of Mann

Manx National Heritage (in Manx 'Eiraght Ashoonagh Vannin' in case you didn't know) has done a great job in recent years resurrecting and popularising the Island's heritage through a number of excellent museums.

A few years ago, the organisation decided to treat the numerous heritage sites on the Island as of equal importance, bringing them together in a unified project called 'The Story of Mann'. This initiative has received great acclaim and Manx National heritage have picked up the British Isles Museum of the Year 1992/93 Prize, the European Museum of the Year 1993 Special Award and a Gulbenkian Museum and Gallery Award in 1992. Encouraged by their success, Manx National Heritage opened in 1997 the latest project, 'House of Manannan' in Peel.

The museums mentioned here are the principal functioning museums on the Island. However, the Story of Mann will lead you to many other historic sites, often in out of the way places. Within the Island's 227 square miles, there are prehistoric monuments, Iron Age hill forts, early Christian chapels, Norse houses, collections of ancient crosses and the outstanding Peel and Rushen castles. From the modern era, there is Tynwald Hill. This is far from being an exhaustive list and you could spend weeks exploring the Island's heritage. There are also Visitor Centres and Nature Trails, all devoted to conservation of the Isle of Man at Scarlett and The Ayres as well as the Tynwald Craft Centre.

House of Manannan

Members of the National Trust, Scottish National Trust, English Heritage and certain overseas trusts note that admission, on production of the appropriate documentation, is free to all those sites where a charge is normally made. There are plenty of maps, guide books and pieces of literature that will help you pick your way around the Island's heritage. The Story of Mann Partners are people who are knowledgeable about the Island's history and you will find them dotted about the Island as staff in hotels, pubs, car rental firms, public transport, ferries and planes. There are Heritage Shops at the Manx Museum and at each of the Story of Mann sites (during the summer season).

The Island's Treasure House

The starting point for The Story of Mann is the Manx Museum on Crellin's Hill in Douglas. The museum contains a great deal of the Island's art treasures and artefacts. There are specialist exhibitions, which change regularly and a comprehensive programme of lectures and films throughout the year. There is a restaurant at the museum and a heritage shop. There is limited parking in front of the museum, but plenty nearby.

For students of history, the modern

research facilities offered by the Museum Library are excellent, particularly for delving into family trees. The Island was fortunate in that much of its written records were saved from the worst excesses of Henry VIII and the Reformation. In the autumn of 1997 the present Earl Derby gifted many of his family's historic papers to Manx National Heritage in microfilm form, which will very much help research into the history of the Island.

Manx Museum

The House of Manannan

The £6 million House of Manannan was opened on the 7th July 1997, by the Irish President Mary Robinson. There is an unlikely and fascinating display of interactive historical displays. You can meet a Celtic Chieftain, experience the peace and tranquillity of an ancient Christian 'Keill' or church, visit a wattle-walled roundhouse, or smell a rich oak-smoked Manx kipper. These are among the diverse experiences awaiting time travellers.

You can wander through the 'Forest of Masts', discover the Manx connections with the Mutiny on the Bounty and delve into the history of the Battle of Jurby when Captain Elliot defeated the French fleet. You can also hear about one of Admiral Lord Nelson's favourite seamen, Captain Quilliam who steered HMS Victory at the battle of Trafalgar. If you fancy commanding your own ship, then visit to the Isle of Man Steam Packet Gallery. And if your maritime interest is in ships of an even earlier age, then have a look at 'Odin's Raven', a two thirds replica Viking longship that was built in Norway during the Island's Millennium of Tynwald year in 1979, and sailed to Peel. Helping you unravel this part of The Story of Mann is the ancient Manx Sea God, Manannan. With the

House of Manannan

Castle Rushen

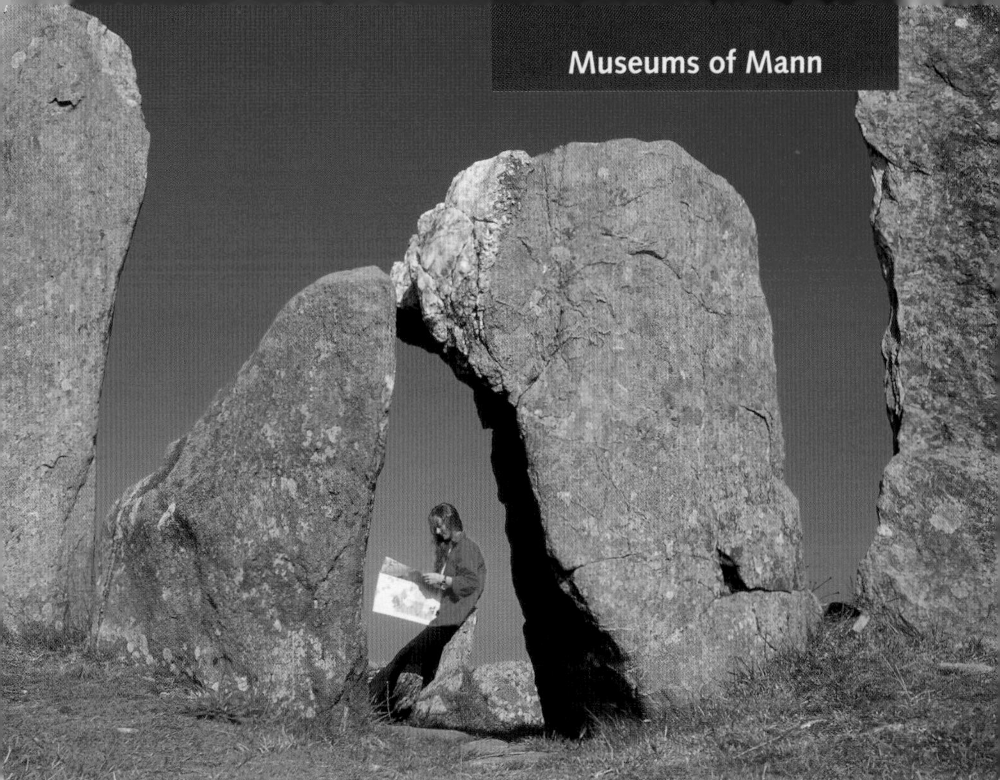

Cashtal yn Ard

clever use of the latest technology, Manannan acts as guide and mentor as you travel backward and forwards through time.

The Peggy Story

The Nautical Museum by Castletown harbour houses many Manx seafaring treasures including the 18th-century armed yacht the "Peggy", discovered by accident in a bricked-up boathouse, 100 years after her owner Captain George Quayle died. The "Peggy" epitomises the days of the smuggling trade. There is a large collection of models and photographs, a replica cabin from the days of Nelson and a fully rigged sail loft.

Scholars and Clergymen

On the south-side of Castletown harbour lies a building constructed around 1200. Built originally as the first church in the Island's old capital, it became a school in later years and now enjoys a new lease of life as a museum. Amongst its displays are many artefacts from school life of yesteryear including a complete re-construction of a Victorian classroom.

The Cregneash Story

Cregneash is the Island's oldest village, situated on the southern peninsula. It is home to an excellent open air museum. With stunning views over Spanish Head and the Calf of Man, it is a popular place to visit. There is much to see around the village so allow time for a good wander. The museum shows life as it was in a 19th-century Manx crofting community. Inside the picturesque whitewashed thatched cottages there are displays showing the old skills employed in that era. There is a café serving home cooked meals and snacks. It is open during the summer months.

Gibbs of the Grove

On the outskirts of Ramsey these buildings house a very fine collection of period furnishings, tools and agricultural machinery, clothes, toys and all that was needed to run the summer household of a wealthy 19th-century shipping magnate. Set in beautiful grounds you can also enjoy the company of a variety of ducks, hens and the friendly Manx cats.

The Great Laxey Wheel

Situated in a prominent position high up on the hillside above the pretty former mining village of Laxey, the Great Laxey Wheel is by repute the largest working water-wheel in the world. It is permanent testimony to the Victorian engineers who built it in 1854, to pump the waste waters from the lower mine workings, up to 2000 feet below. Named "Lady Isabella" in honour of the wife of a former Lieutenant Governor, the wheel was capable of drawing water at the rate of 250 gallons per minute and disposing of it through a clever system of channels to the washing floors further down the valley. It still works and if you have a head for heights then climb the steps to the viewing platform at the top of its 72 ft-diameter. The vista is well worth the effort.

Castle Rushen

Laxey

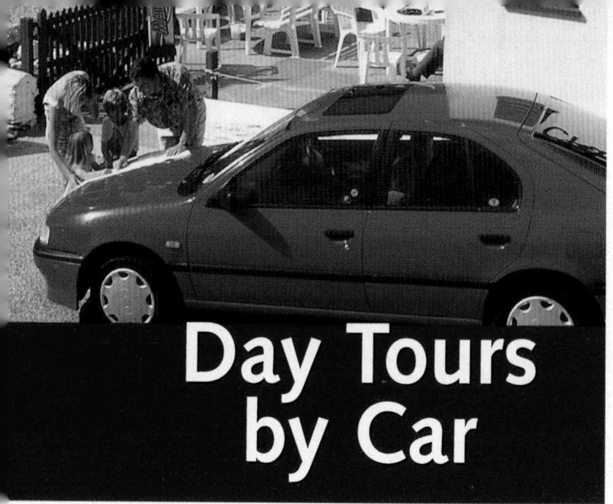

Day Tours by Car

Although not the most environmentally sound way to discover the Isle of Man – nor, for that matter, the best way to see the Island in detail – many readers, particularly those who have difficulty in getting around, will choose to tour the Island by car, hence this section of the guide.

However, if you can use foot, bicycle or horseback to explore the Isle of Man, go for one of these options – not only will you see much more, you'll also be helping the environment!

If you don't have your own vehicle there are several car hire firms on the Island. Arrangements can be made to meet you at the Sea Terminal or to deliver a car to your hotel or accommodation.

Double and single yellow lines have precisely the same meaning as in the UK and elsewhere. You can pick up a parking disc on board any of the Isle of Man Steam Packet vessels, the Sea Terminal, Airport, Car Hire companies, Police Stations or from the local Commissioners Offices.

The Routes

The routes chosen cover most regions in the Isle of Man and are designed to be enjoyed at a leisurely pace, giving ample opportunity to visit points of interest along the way. The accompanying maps should be sufficient for the purpose, but more detailed information can of course be found on the Ordnance Survey Map of the Isle of Man. Please bear in mind that although the country areas are well served by petrol stations, there are districts where they are spaced a good distance apart.

Tour 1

Douglas: Signpost Corner: The Bungalow: Ramsey: Maughold: Port Mooar: Port Cornaa: Dhoon: Laxey. 35 miles.

This tour starts at the foot of Broadway, which is adjacent to the Villa Marina or just about where the Harris Promenade merges with Central Promenade.

Climbing up Broadway you leave the tourist part of town behind and as Broadway becomes Ballaquayle Road you come to the Bray Hill traffic lights - turn right and head past the TT Grandstand (on your right). Some three quarters of a mile along Glencrutchery Road you arrive at Governor's Bridge. Be careful here that you don't turn too quickly, and take care at the double roundabout before following the road marked

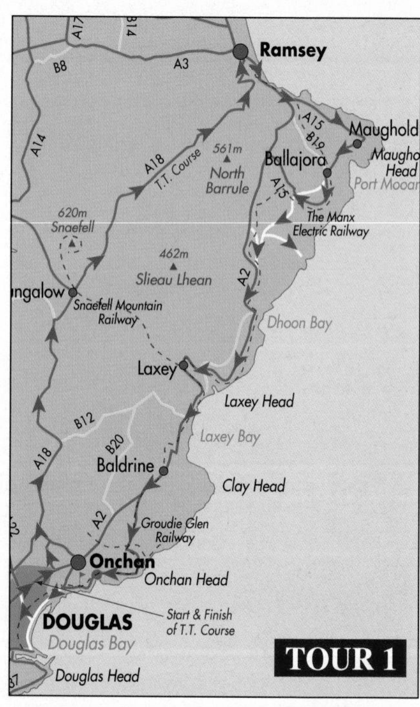

Ramsey, turning up - left - by the white painted stone wall. For the next few hundred yards on the right you are passing the home of the Island's Governor. Head on up the A18 to Signpost Corner. Leaving Cronk-ny-Mona behind there is a distinct change of scenery starting to take place as the road winds upwards to the famous TT viewing spot of Creg-ny-Baa. Over to your left as Kate's Cottage comes into sight are some very good views of Douglas and the panorama of the southern half of the Isle of Man lies before you. Please be very careful where you stop to view, especially on the TT Course as it is a very fast road. Passing through Keppel Gate you are now in the mountains and into some of the finest scenery on the Island.

Still on the A18 descend to Ramsey at Brandywell, just past the junction with the B10. Directly in front of you stands Snaefell and if time permits it is well worth stopping

Ramsey

here and catching an electric tram to the summit. On a clear day seven kingdoms can be seen from the summit - England, Wales, Scotland, Ireland, Mann, the Kingdom of the Sea ... and the Kingdom of Heaven. In 1995 the Snaefell Mountain railway celebrated its centenary with the original rolling stock still in use. Past Snaefell the magnificent mountain scenery continues with the views on your right of Laxey and its valley gradually giving way to the impressive sight of Ramsey and the northern plain spreading out before you. Ramsey is well worth exploring ... and if you have still not picked up your free parking disc, call in at Ramsey Town Hall, they will fix you up.

Maughold is the next stop. Drive along Ramsey Promenade and past the Queen's Pier, watching for the signs directing traffic to Laxey A2. Shortly after bear left onto the A15. A good tip on these roads is to watch out for the un-manned tram crossings as you

Maughold lighthouse

will be criss-crossing them for the next few miles. About half a mile past Maughold there is a small road which takes you down onto the peaceful beach at Port Mooar. It's an ideal place to stretch your legs and have a picnic. Back up from the beach turn left onto the A15 and travel to Cornaa.

There is a well preserved burial ground just past the Ballajora crossroads - look for an old chapel on the corner, keep that to the left and travel up hill on the minor road - which in more recent times became the last resting place for those Quakers who remained on the Island, the majority of their fellow believers escaping persecution by seeking a new life in America. Take care approaching Cornaa as the roads are very narrow. Turn off the A15 at Cornaa tram halt and turn down the minor road to the left. Pass the Ballaglass Glen car park on your right and drive on until you reach a small ford where you turn sharp right for Port Cornaa. The drive down to the beach is well worth the effort, but be careful where you park, it is a popular spot with locals and sometimes the stony upper beach can cause problems if you pick the wrong place.

When coming back up this lovely wooded valley continue past the ford - on your right - and climb back up onto the A2 watching out for the signs to the Dhoon and Laxey. If you are feeling energetic park opposite the Dhoon station and enjoy a walk down to the shore, but remember to leave extra time for the return journey ... it can fool you. The A2 soon takes you to Laxey and there are great views all along the coast.

There is a choice on how you leave Laxey. If you are in Old Laxey then the steep road up from the harbour soon comes out on the A2 at Fairy Cottage, or if you have been exploring around the mines then rejoin by the Electric Railway station. On through the picturesque villages of Lonan, Garwick and Baldrine and over the tram crossing just out of Baldrine, taking a left turn and over a second crossing in the vicinity of the Halfway House to Laxey (Liverpool Arms) - the road A11 is signposted to Groudle and Douglas. Groudle has a beautiful natural glen and the revitalised miniature Groudle Railway.

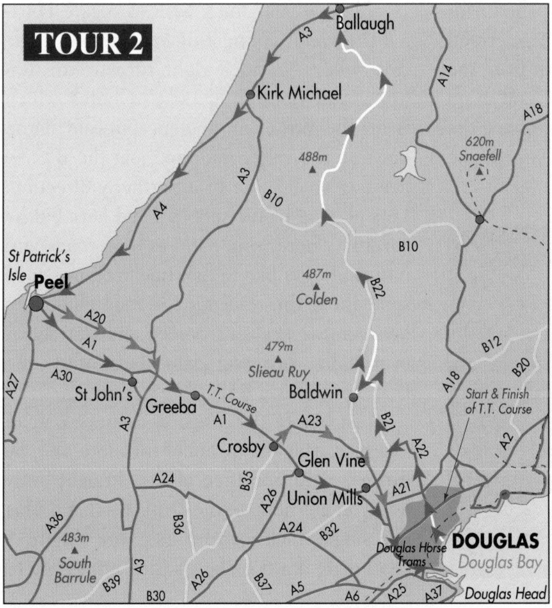

Tour 2

Douglas: East Baldwin: Injebreck: Druidale: Ballaugh: Kirk Michael: Peel: St. John's. 38 miles

This journey takes as its starting point the bottom of Broadway and proceeds in just the same manner as that described in Tour 1, until the traffic lights at Parkfield Corner (St. Ninians Church) are reached. Get into the filter left lane and enjoy the run down Bray Hill to the bottom of the dip where you take a right turn. TT racers speed down this hill at over 150 mph!

The road now winds along through an area known as Port-e-Chee, which translated from the Gaelic means Haven of Peace. Cronkbourne Village is the next destination and this is soon reached. Turn right and go up the steep Johnny Watterson's Lane A21 turning left at the halt sign, then drive along Ballanard Road A22 towards Abbeylands for just over a mile. At the crossroads turn left and heading over Sir George's Bridge make a right turn onto the B21, the East Baldwin Road.

Between 1900-05 a narrow three foot gauge railway wound its way around these small valleys, carrying workers and building materials for the Injebreck Reservoir. Keep on the B21 and move in a northerly direction until you reach the old and disused East Baldwin Chapel. Park here awhile and see if you can spot "The White Man of East Baldwin". The "White Man" is a figure built into a mountain wall on the hillside as a memorial to a Deemster, who perished with his horse in a snowstorm whilst on an errand of mercy. The walk up to the cairn from the bottom of the valley is strenuous, and mind you don't get your feet wet when crossing the Baldwin River, but the views are worth the effort.

Sulby Glen

Sulby Reservoir

Retrace your track back to Algare Hill - it's the small connecting road between the two valleys - and a right turn at the top brings you along to St Luke's Church which is on the site of an ancient Tynwald. Drop down to the valley floor and join the B22 by heading once more in a northerly direction. Lots of good picnic spots around here but be careful where you park as the roads are narrow. If you like to fish Injebreck is a good spot. From the reservoir the road climbs up between the peaks of Colden and Carraghan eventually bringing you out onto the Brandywell Road B10.

Just before the junction there is a small slip road which you should turn into and, by turning right and then almost straight away left, you are now on the Druidale Road. This is a single track road for its entire length. A short drive down Ballaugh Glen brings you to the village.

Turning left at the famous Ballaugh Bridge – where TT racers become airborne for some distance – you head south west towards Kirk Michael, home of runic crosses and the last resting place of five bishops. Take the right fork here as the A3 becomes the A4 and head down towards Peel. This is a good road, but if you are not in a hurry stop off at Glen Wyllin, Glen Mooar or the Devil's Elbow.

It's worth spending some time in Peel. This is the only "city" on the Island, with two cathedrals, and there are some interesting shops, narrow streets, a harbour and a very fine castle. If you are out on an evening run, stay for the sunset, you won't be disappointed. Leaving Peel behind take the A1 to St. John's, a village of great political importance to the Island. An alternative route to the village is via the A20 and the connecting road through Tynwald Mills, which is well signposted from Peel. Alongside Tynwald Hill lies the Royal Chapel of St. John. The village is little changed in the best part of a century.

The last part of the drive takes you along the central valley. Ten thousand years ago this was the sea bed, dividing the two main parts of the Isle of Man from each other. Moving along the A1 towards Ballacraine you come up against an Island rarity - a set of traffic lights. Carry straight on towards Douglas, but just after Greeba Castle look to your left and there is the ancient roofless church of St. Trinian standing in splendid isolation in its own meadow.

There is a choice of routes to the capital from here on. The main road follows the A1 to the Sea Terminal via Glen Vine, Union Mills, Braddan Bridge, and the Quarter Bridge. Alternatively if time permits why not take the A23, the Nab Road, by turning left at Crosby and heading towards Douglas via Eyreton, the Nab, the Strang and Braddan - the A23 rejoins the A1 at the Jubilee Oak Braddan Bridge.

Tour 3

Ramsey: Point of Ayre: Jurby: The Cronk: The Curraghs: Sulby: Tholt-e-Will: The Bungalow. 38 Miles

As you wander around the northern plain the scenery changes frequently, from the fine sands of the Lhen, gravel beaches of the Point of Ayre, up to the wooded slopes of Sky Hill, Glen Auldyn, Carrick, Rock and Mount Karrin, St. Ciaran's Mount. Coupled with the winding lanes of the Curraghs it is one of the best places to tour. The drive starts on Ramsey Promenade, but before setting off be sure to take in the lovely sight of the bay and the slopes of Liargee Frissel, Frissel's slope - it's the hill with the tower set on the summit.

Driving along the Mooragh Promenade you may get a glimpse of St. Bee's Head in Cumberland, the nearest mainland point to the Isle of Man. At the end of the promenade bear left up the hill and join the A10 by turning right. Follow this road to the lovely

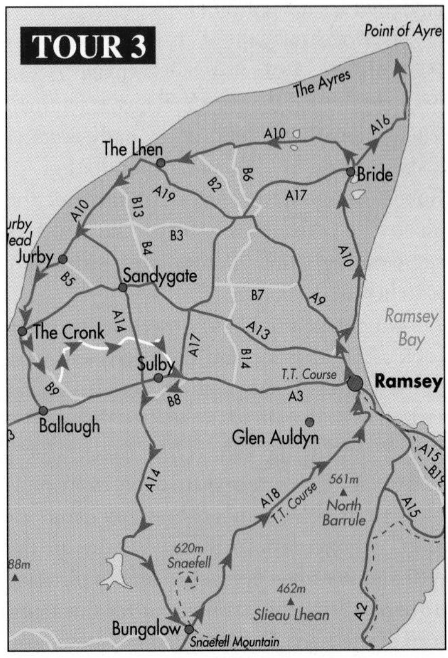

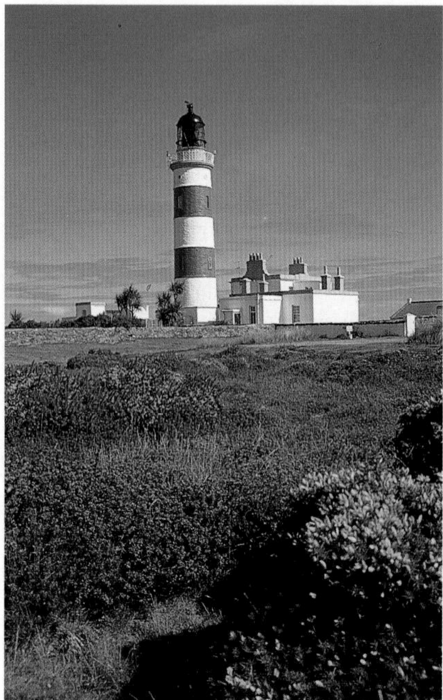

Point of Ayre Lighthouse

village of Bride. The church acts as a good landmark for miles around.

At Bride take the A16 marked for the Point of Ayre. Again it is an easy place to find because the lighthouse stands as a sentinel. This landmark was built in the early years of last century by the great-grandfather of Robert Louis Stevenson. Definitely not the place to go swimming, the waters surrounding the Point are extremely treacherous.

On now to the Lhen, so reverse the route back as far as Bride and turn right and west at the church. Lovely country here with good farming land rolling down to the coast. Watch out for the sign to the Ayres Visitor Centre, well worth a visit; open from mid-May to mid-September between from 2-5pm., Wednesdays to Sundays. Stay on the A10 and the Lhen is reached after a pleasant drive of a few miles. Watch out for the sharp turn at the Lhen Bridge. The little park close to the shore is ideal for a picnic.

Just a couple of miles further on is Jurby. This village long ago was important for the Vikings and although it has lost something of its old eminence it is nonetheless a pleasant part of the Island, and well worth exploring for its beaches, church and crosses. Carrying on still further on the A10 look out for The Cronk, The Hill, such as it is. Go straight on here at the crossroads following the B9 and turn left at the second road down from The Cronk crossroads ... don't count any farm tracks or lanes. If you have got it right, it should be the yellow coloured road on the map taking you towards Dollagh Mooar, Black Lake and the Curraghs, Mire or Marsh. Caution here because the roads are extremely narrow and there are lots of ditches awaiting the careless driver. Cross the A14, approximately half way between Sandygate to the north and Sulby to the south - and you are still following the yellow road to Kella and West Sulby.

Turn left at the junction and for a brief distance you are on the TT course on the famous Sulby Straight A3. Just past Sulby Bridge is the Ginger Hall public house and you should turn right here onto the B8 which will fetch you onto the Sulby Claddaghs, the River Meadowland. Drive through the Claddaghs to the A14 or the Sulby Glen Road and begin the ascent of the glen towards Tholt-e-Will. This extremely

Manx countryside in the autumn

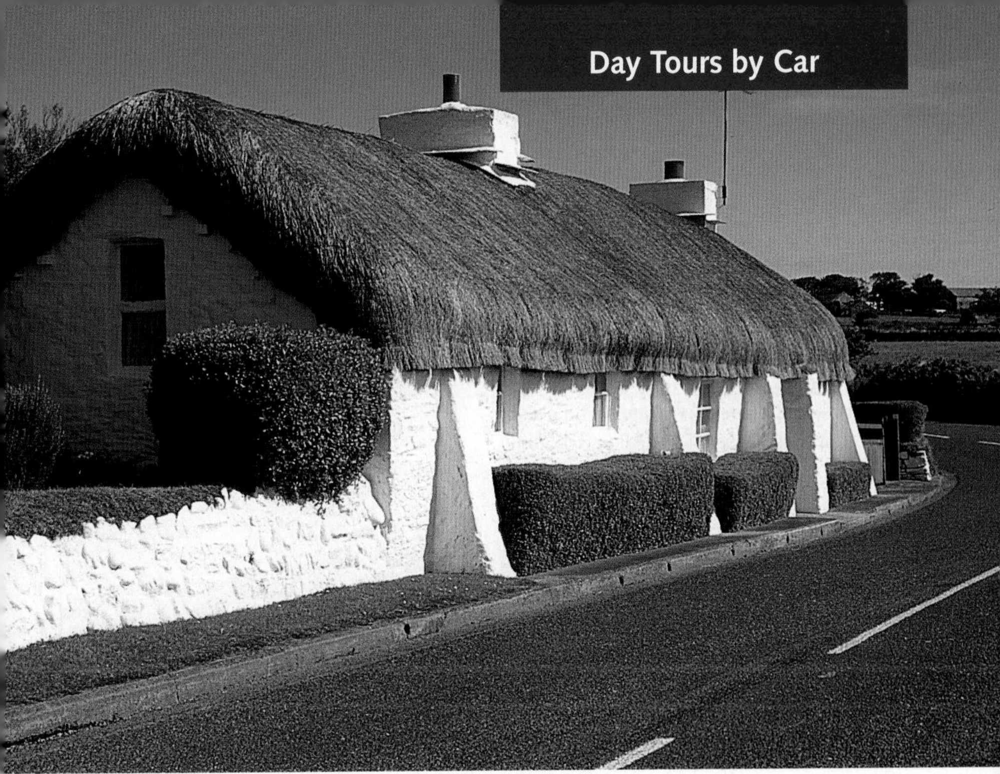

A Manx Thatched Cottage

scenic route brings you up past the Sulby Reservoir built in the early eighties with the aim of securing water supplies well into the 21st century. The upper reaches of the road roll across the shoulder of Snaefell and the scenery is typical of high moorland interspersed with plantation.

The end of the A14 joins the A18 TT course at the Bungalow. There is an Electric Railway station here and during the season the Snaefell Mountain Railway operates regular services between Snaefell summit and Laxey far below at the bottom of the valley. Turn left and travel the "wrong way" around the TT course, it is still a fast stretch of road. In clear weather, summer or winter, there are fine views of the Ayres, Scotland, England and Ireland. Please take care on the final descent into Ramsey, there are some sharp corners. Once into Royal Ramsey the final destination is yours, it is an easy town to find your way about and the A18 takes you right into Parliament Square. Turn right just through the Square and you are into Derby Road and West Quay. Cross the Swing Bridge and onto Mooragh Promenade.

Tour 4

Peel: St. John's: Cronk-y-Voddy: West Baldwin: Ballasalla: Castletown: Foxdale. 40 miles.

Peel is a must for all visitors and if you are not actually staying there then a visit should be a priority. Tour 4 will take you from Peel through the Island's lovely hinterland, taking in moorland, valleys and glens. The starting point is the north end of Peel Promenade in the vicinity of the Empire Garage. From here proceed up Stanley Road turning right then almost immediately left into Church Street. At the halt sign - the Peel Police Station is across the road - take a left and head into Derby Road and the A20 signposted for St. John's. You will know that you have the right road when you pass the Poortown quarry and after about a mile and a half, turn right down the small road marked Tynwald Craft Centre, which is well worth a visit.

Leave the Tynwald Craft Centre complex by the opposite end and bear left onto the TT course, the A3. The exit onto the main road is narrow and sometimes approaching cars from your right hand side may be travelling at speed. Now you are heading up the beautiful wooded Glen Helen road and if you feel like stretching your legs, stop and stroll up the glen. From opposite the glen car park the road climbs steeply for a short distance passing the famous TT landmark Sarah's Cottage, on up Creg Willeys Hill, Willy Syl's or Sylvester's Crag and on to Cronk-y-Voddy, which translated from the Manx means the Hill of the Dog. Here at the crossroads turn right for the undulating drive to Little London.

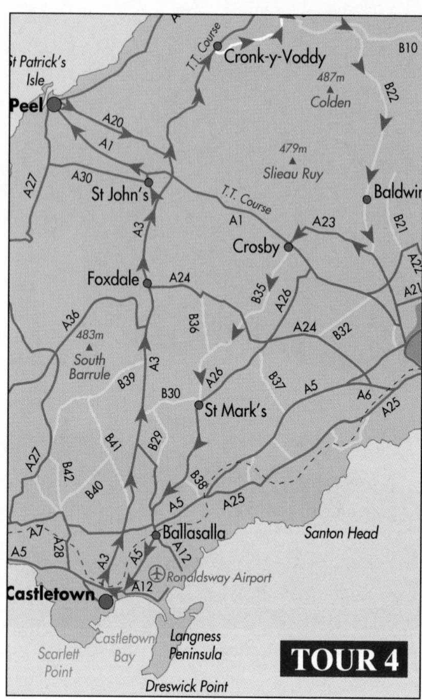

Little London long ago was famous for fishing but nowadays its peace and tranquillity is only disturbed by the occasional passing car or walker. Before WW11, the Old Smithy was the home of the famous flyer Captain Pixton who was the first British winner of the prestigious Schneider Trophy and the holder of many flying records. The road out of Little London skirts the south west slopes of Sartfell, which is old Norse for Black Mountain or Dark Slope. In Manx it is known as Slieau Dhoo and joins the B10 about half a mile above Bayr Garrow, Rough Road.

Just before the minor road joins the main road is Sartfield Farmhouse Restaurant. The views from here are superb and at night you can see various Irish and Scottish lighthouses.

Turn up the hill and on the way look back at the view; on clear days there are fine panoramas of the Mountains of Mourne and the Mull of Galloway. You are now heading along the Brandywell Road with Colden Mountain ahead and to the right. There are a lot of cattle grids in the mountains, so be sure to take care crossing them and if you have to use the gates, please don't forget to close them after use. Keep a look out for the B22 turning; it should be easy to spot because it is just before Brandywell Cottage, and that is the only building on the left since

Looking towards St John's

Castletown

you started on the B10. Turn off to the right and head along the Injebreck Road, and if you want a good idea of what the centre of the Island looks like, pull in just before the crest of the hill and you will see a countryside little changed in thousands of years.

Heading down into the West Baldwin valley – an area not unlike the Scottish Highlands. At the upper end of this green and tree lined cleft is Carraghan, which translates in English to rough, craggy or rocky place. It was chosen as an ideal spot for the Injebreck Reservoir which has served Douglas and much of the Island for many decades. On down the valley, keep to the B22 all the way until Mount Rule halt sign, where a right turn puts you onto the A23 bound for the central village of Crosby. The road follows what was the edge of the south coast of the larger of the two northern islands that made up the Isle of Man at the time of the last Ice Age.

Go straight across the Crosby crossroads and up the B35 towards St Mark's. It is likely that at one time a cross stood somewhere near the site of the present day village, because its name is derived from the Scandinavian word for Cross Village or Farm. The tour now follows one of the driveable parts of the Millennium Way.

St Mark's is a quiet little backwater and lies peacefully on a rise and visible for a good distance around the parish of Malew. Once a year it comes to life with the holding of the ancient St Mark's Fair. A couple of miles or so further on you come to the busy village of Ballasalla. In more recent times there has been an upsurge in commercial activities here. There is plenty to do in Ballasalla, including a visit to Silverdale Glen, which is well signposted.

Go straight on at each roundabout looking for the Airport and Castletown signs, the A5. Pass the airport on your left and drive into Castletown. The old capital is described in detail elsewhere and it is well worth a visit. This is a disc parking area.

The journey back to Peel is fairly straight forward. Retrace the route back along the harbour in Castletown to Victoria Road and the first roundabout, where you should turn left into Alexander Road, crossing over the Alexander Bridge. Carry on for a quarter of a mile and turn right into Malew Road and the A3. Stay on the A3, climbing up the Ballamodha Straight before dropping down through the old mining villages of Upper and Lower Foxdale. Approaching St John's the road divides at a small hamlet called The Hope (not shown on many maps) take the left branch and follow the A30 past the Forestry Dept.'s nurseries, bearing right until you reach the halt sign in the middle of the village. A good guide if you are on the correct route is that Tynwald Hill is across the road. Turn left at St John's for Peel and follow the A1 and the signs all the way to Peel Promenade and the end of Tour 4.

Tour 5

Port Erin: The Slogh: Niarbyl: Glen Maye: Foxdale: Braaid: Union Mills: Douglas: Ballasalla: Port St. Mary: Cregneash. 42 miles

Port Erin is a good place to base yourself for a motoring holiday. Parking is easy and although parts of the village are disc zones, they present no real problems.

This drive starts on the Upper Promenade and covers the southern part of the Island. It takes you from the steep cliffs and hills of the south west, through the gentle rolling hills of Glenfaba, Rushen and Middle Sheadings to the Capital, and on to the old Manx hill village of Cregneash.

Drive up the hill away from the hotels and look for the signposts to Bradda. The village nestles on the slopes of Bradda Head and is divided into west and east, although the exact boundary between them is now somewhat blurred. This is the A32 and it

Port Erin

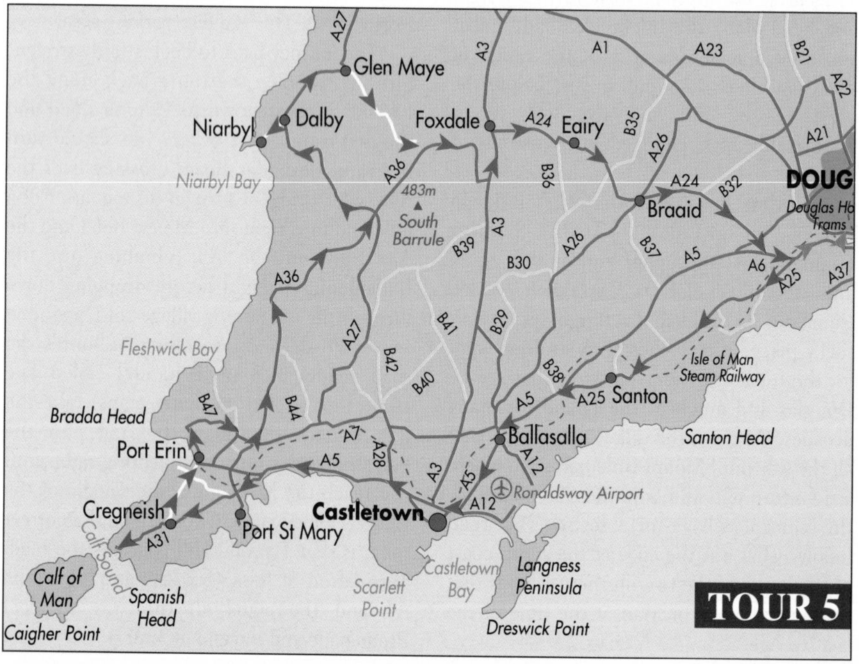

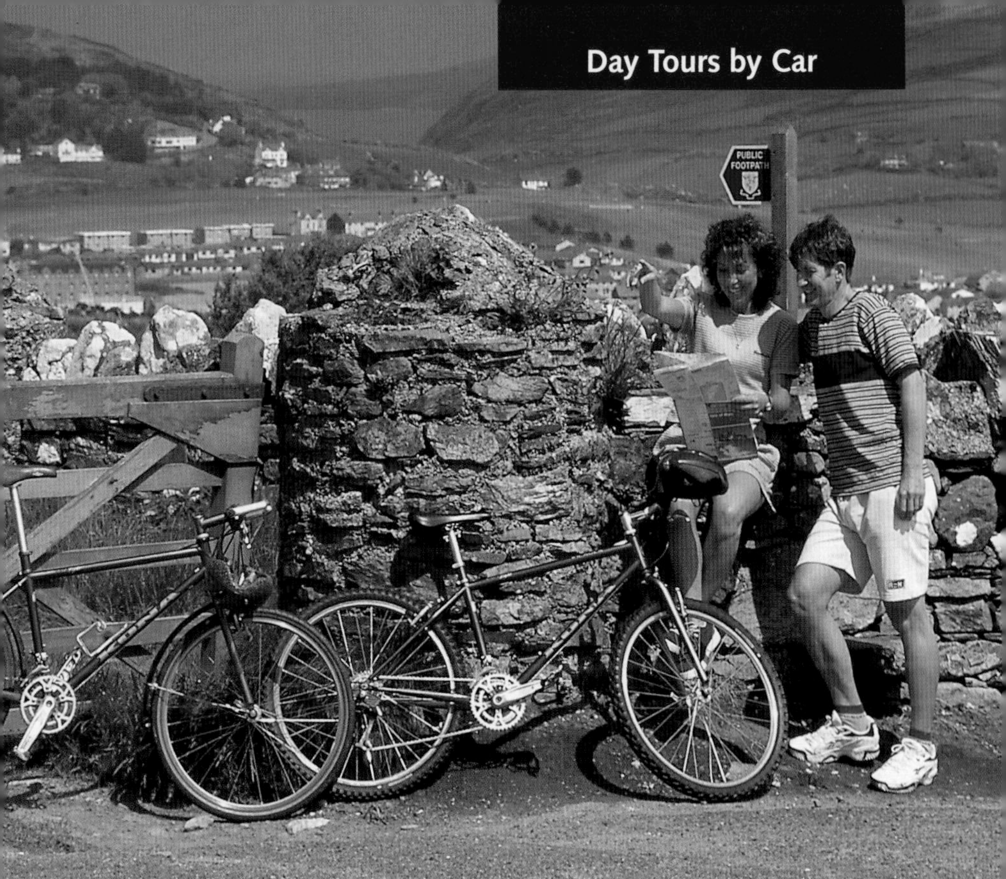

Cycling near Port Erin

brings you along a gradually widening road to Ballafesson, which appears on the ancient manorial roll as MacPherson's Farm. At the junction you pick up the A7 for a short while and at the next crossroads - marked as a roundabout - turn left on the A36, up through Ballakillowey, McGillowey's Farm. It should be noted that the Manx usually exchanged the prefix Mac for the prefix Balla as far as place names were concerned. Just before the junction with the B44 is reached there is a nice open picnic area, with fine views over Castletown Bay, and the sweep of the coast right round to the villages of The Howe and Cregneash high up on the Mull Peninsula.

Driving on upwards on the Slogh Road, there are continually changing views of the landscape around almost every corner. There are many fine walks and picnic sites.

The Sloc Road takes you to the Round Table crossroads. Turn sharp left here onto the A27 and down to Niarbyl. Descending the hill into Dalby village, it is easy to see where the name Niarbyl is derived. Jutting out into the clear waters of the Irish Sea is a tail of rocks, which is how Niarbyl translates into English. Take the minor road down to the shore and spend some time on the rocky beach at the foot of the cliffs.

From Dalby the A27 continues on to Glen Maye, loosely translated meaning Yellow Glen on account of the muddy, almost clay coloured waters of the streams running down the glen - there are a number of easy walks here.

From here carry on to the village post office. To the side of the building there is a narrow country lane which takes you up towards Garey, translated as rough or rugged river-shrubbery. Up here on the high ground, if there ever was a river, it has long since disappeared - perhaps the road was the river, because in wet winter weather the road does seem to double as a stream. The road is also known as the Back of the Moon Road.

Rushen Mines soon loom up and even the isolation of the mines has a particular beauty of its own. Back onto the A36 with a left turn and down the mountain to South Barrule Plantation and the junction with the A3. Head left towards Foxdale where you take the first right and join the A24. Skirt the edge of the Eairy Dam - watch out for the ducks crossing the road - and on to The Braaid - literally translated it means throat or windpipe as applied in the sense of a glen or sheltered vale. Carry straight on at the roundabout, head up the hill about half a mile, and look down and across into the central valley to the view known as the Plains of Heaven.

Carry on this road until you arrive at a major road junction where the A24 bisects the A5, cross over and drive to Kewaigue, which translates into Little Hollow. If you would like to re-visit Douglas, continue on into town, if not then just past the Isle of Man Breweries headquarters, turn through an acute right hander and head for Santon on the A25. Santon - in older times it was spelt Santan - derives its name from Saint Sanctan. This road is known as the Old Castletown Road and there are a number of roads leading off it down to rocky bays and isolated coves. Try them when you have time, most are off the beaten track and are not accessible by public transport. The road takes you in the direction of Ballasalla and rejoins the A5 at a spot where the railway line passes under the main road. Stay on the A5 by turning left at the Ballasalla roundabout - the Whitestone Inn faces you directly ahead as you approach it.

Drive past the airport and skirt the edge of Castletown. Leave the town behind by using the bypass, it's still the A5, drive all the way along the edge of Bay ny Carrickey, The Bay of the Rock, and turn right up past the tall stone building along Beach Road, heading for the crossroads, where you go straight on using the A31. Ignore any other roads and make for Cregneash. From here carry on down to The Calf Sound to enjoy the totally unspoiled scenery of the Isle of Man's equivalent of Land's End.

For the final stages of the drive you return back up the hill from The Sound towards Cregneash again. Just before entering the village from the south, turn sharp left onto the minor road leading past Mull Hill and its stone circles. Dating from Neolithic times, this unspoilt area remains much as the earliest inhabitants would have known it. This is a single track road with passing places. Port Erin nestles quietly below as you drive down Dandy Hill and onto the Lower Promenade.

Tour 6

Onchan: Baldrine: Laxey: Glen Roy: The Bungalow: Sulby: St. Judes: Andreas: Bride: Ramsey: The Gooseneck: The Hibernian: Dhoon: Laxey. 49 miles.

Onchan started life as a small village to the north of Douglas and has in recent times seen a growth outstripping that of the modern day capital. You could be forgiven for thinking that it is a suburb of Douglas, but the village has its own local government and is very much a separate community.

The drive starts at Onchan Head, just above Port Jack. Follow the A11 as it runs parallel to the tram track, passing as you go Groudle Glen. There is a minor road off to the right, approximately half a mile past Groudle Station and a detour up this road will bring you to Old Kirk Lonan Church, well worth a visit. Completing the detour brings you out onto the A2 just to the south of Baldrine village. Carry on towards Laxey via Fairy Cottage and Old Laxey Hill - bear to the right at the filling station – to the attractive harbour.

Laxey owes its origins to the Norsemen who named it Salmon River. Give yourself time here as there's plenty to see. From the harbour travel up the glen besides the river and when you reach the woollen mills, go up the hill, under the railway bridge and straight on at the stop sign looking for the Creg-ny-Baa signpost. You are now on the Glen Roy Road (coloured yellow on the OS map) and about to experience one of the best glen drives on the Island. The glen was formed by the waters cascading down from Mullagh

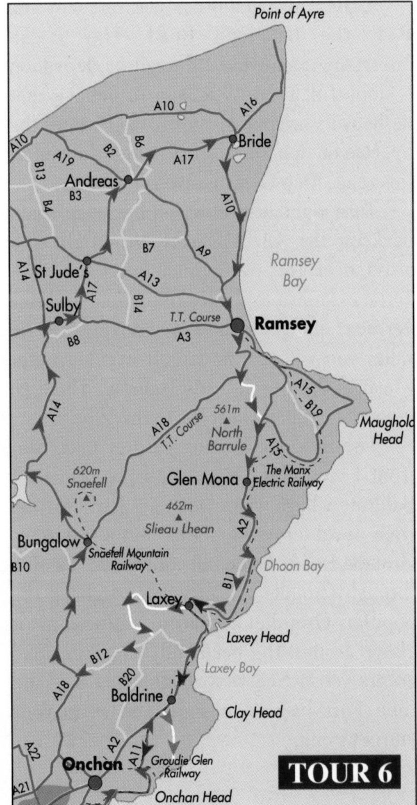

Snaefell Mountain Railway

Ouyr, Slieau Meayll, Dun Summit, Bare or Bald Mountain and Windy Corner respectively. Look out for the Ballalheannagh Gardens they are well worth a visit. Care on this road is required as there are a number of blind corners, and the road is extremely narrow in places.

Eventually you rejoin a wider road, the B12 just above Social Cottage, and by turning in a south west (right) direction, the road brings you to the well known Keppel Hotel at Creg-ny-Baa. Turn right and head the "wrong way" round the TT course, the A18, aiming for the Bungalow. Just past Brandywell is the highest point on the course at almost 1,400 feet.

The Bungalow actually bears no resemblance to a modern building of that name and the current site was home, until fairly recently, to a magnificent hotel made of wood and galvanised sheeting - very popular with TT fans. Watch out for the directions to Sulby and turn left on the A14.

If your passengers fancy a walk, pull up at the top entrance to Tholt-e-Will Glen. Give them half an hour or so to walk down the glen and pick them up just outside the inn at the bottom of the hill. Alternatively Sulby Reservoir car park makes a good location for a picnic. The name of the glen translated from the Manx means Hill of the Cattlefold, and the inhabitants of the lower end of the bigger glen have traditionally been known as the Sulby Cossacks. At any time of the year, Sulby Glen has a beauty all of its own. In the spring the east side of the glen colours itself with a haze of bluebells. At other times the heather and gorse lend their own particular splash of colour and always the light creates a special atmosphere.

A quarter of the way down the glen from the inn lies Irishman's Cottage and, high above the nearby waterworks, is the small feeder reservoir of Block Eary. The reservoir was built German POW's and although it is a strenuous walk to reach it, it's well worthwhile. The name has changed somewhat from the original Scandinavian spelling Blakkarg but the meaning is still the same, Black Sheiling, from the peaty colour of the stream.

Carry on down the valley towards the Sulby Straight. Passing Sulby Mill go straight on to the main road and turn right onto the TT Course at Sulby Methodist Church. At the end of the Straight turn off the A3 onto the St Judes Road, the A17. From the West Craig crossroads stay on the A17 to Andreas. There is a subtle change in the scenery here as the land changes from moor and glen to low lying, well drained marsh land.

Andreas has a fine church dedicated to Saint Andrew from whom the parish takes its name. The village is very much the centre of local agricultural activities. Leave Andreas by continuing on the same road which takes you to the Island's northernmost centre of population, Bride. The village lies in a little hollow of the Bride Hills and is one of the sunniest places on the Isle of Man.

Leaving Bride travel along the A10 in the direction of Ramsey The Bride road takes you right into Parliament Square and if you are not breaking your journey in Ramsey then carry on following the route marked for the TT Course and Douglas. High above the town at the Gooseneck there is a minor road leading off behind the TT Marshals' shelter. Careful negotiation of the turn is required to get onto what is known as the Hibernian Road. This is a delightful run across the lower slopes of North Barrule and whilst there seems to be no trace of the name's origination, it is most likely that it takes its form from the same meaning as South Barrule, Ward Mountain.

As you come off this road at the Hibernian, turn right onto the A2, the Coast Road, and head for the Corrany. This name is a variation of Cornaa which means Treen, the modern version of homestead. At the Dhoon, Fort Quarterland, and probably taking its name from the nearby earthworks of Kionehenin, The Head of the Precipice, you can stop and if your passengers are annoying you send them to Onchan by tram.

Leave the Dhoon car park area by the B11, the Ballaragh Road. This is an interesting name and although its derivation is doubtful, there is reason to believe that perhaps its original meaning was Farm of the Spectre or Apparition. Just before the end of this road, King Orry's Grave is reached.

Turn right here and you are once again back on the A2. At Laxey, turn right and cross over the tram lines into Dumbell's Terrace, known to the locals as Ham and Egg Terrace, and park the car. Looking up the valley you will see the largest working water wheel in the world, 'Lady Isabella'. There is, in fact, a car park adjacent to the Wheel.

The final leg of your journey takes you from Laxey along the A2 to just south of Baldrine village where you veer left after the tram level crossing lights onto the A11, Groudle Road (watch out for trams!). Passing through Groudle you may catch sight of the popular Groudle miniature railway as it chugs around the headland. Soon the road grants you a fine view of Douglas Bay and then Port Jack is in sight and so is your journey's end.

Walking on Mann

The Isle of Man has a number of long walks - perhaps the most interesting is the coastal footpath which can normally be done over about five days. The following walks are based on the longer paths but have been split into day walks or less so that less serious walkers can enjoy some of the Island's most beautiful scenery.

Wherever you walk you should wear suitable shoes, or preferably walking boots, particularly on the cliff paths where wet grass can be very slippery and catch out even the most experienced walker. To dress appropriately for the weather is essential and although you will never be far from civilisation some of the coastal areas are exposed and you can get very wet before reaching shelter. The Public Rights of Way Map of the Island published by the Isle of Man Government is an ideal companion and contains a wealth of information.

Many of the place names in the Island are in Manx Gaelic or a corrupted form of it and often describe very aptly either the shape or some other feature of the place. Others describe the origins of the place in relation to the family name of the historical owner. The remaining names have their origins in Norse and date from the Viking Period. Where appropriate the English translation is given to add interest and a better understanding of the place name.

The walks start with the Coastal Footpath which was given the Celtic name of Raad ny Foillan (The Road of the Gull)and opened in 1986 along with the Bayr ny Skeddan (The Herring Road). Together they formed part of the Government's contribution to the Heritage Year celebrations.

The Raad ny Foillan embraces most of the Island's dramatic coastal paths mixed with some unusual rural walks and the vast beach walks of the northern alluvial plain. The total length of the path is around 95 miles depending on the various options open to you along the way. It can be walked at a comfortable pace in a week by serious walkers finding accommodation at the main towns en route. It can also be walked in sections by using public transport and based on central accommodation, which is how it will be described.

The first seven walks make up the Raad ny Foillan but each is a full day walk and you should use public transport to get you to the start or to return from the finish. It is

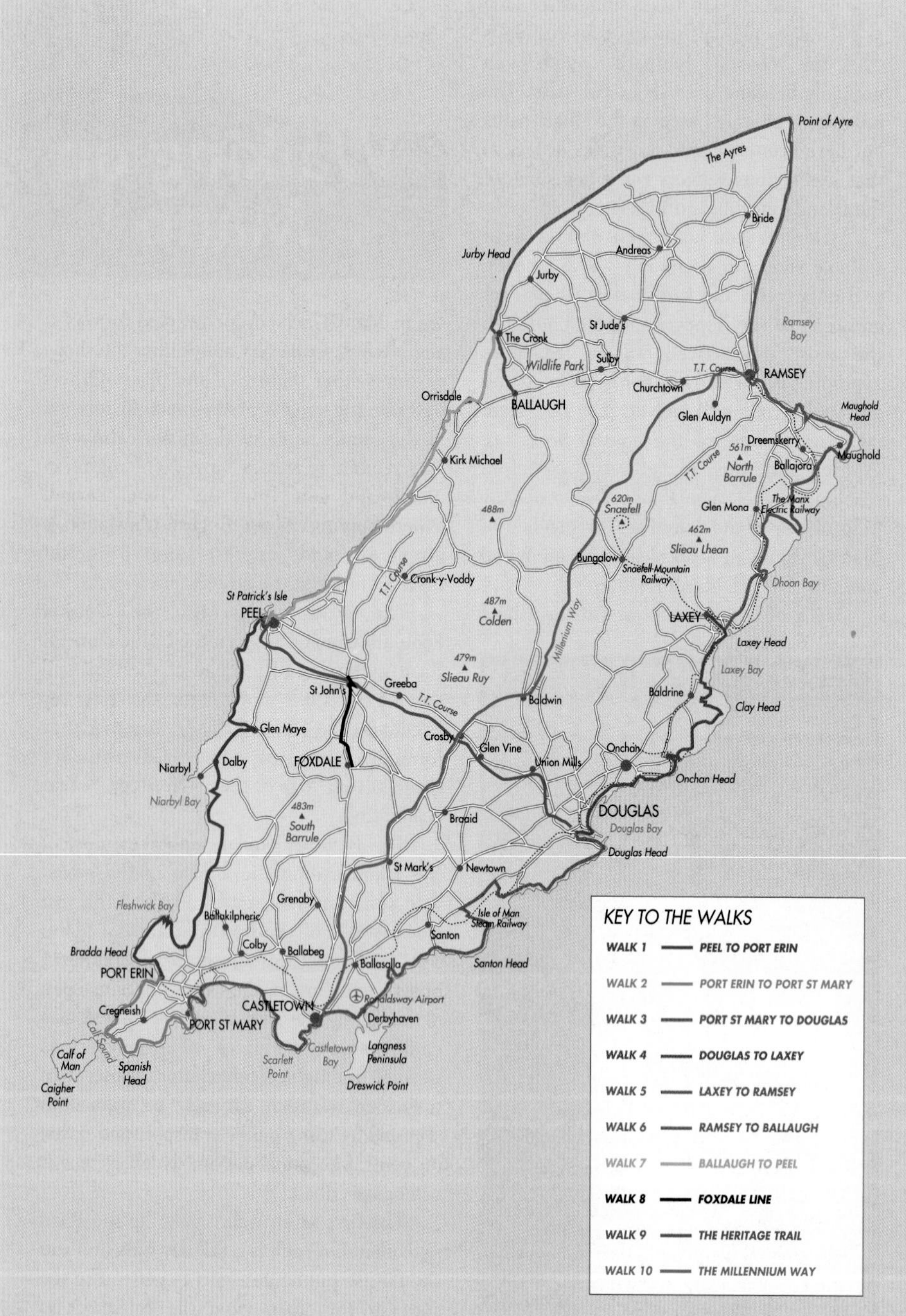
Point of Ayre
The Ayres
Bride
Andreas
Jurby Head
Jurby
St Jude's
Ramsey Bay
The Cronk
Wildlife Park
Sulby
T.T. Course
RAMSEY
Churchtown
Orrisdale
BALLAUGH
Glen Auldyn
Maughold Head
Dreemskerry
561m
North Barrule
Maughold
Kirk Michael
Ballajora
T.T. Course
620m
Snaefell
488m
Glen Mona
The Manx Electric Railway
462m
Slieau Lhean
Bungalow
Snaefell Mountain Railway
Dhoon Bay
T.T. Course
Cronk-y-Voddy
St Patrick's Isle
PEEL
487m
Colden
Millenium Way
LAXEY
Laxey Head
479m
Slieau Ruy
Laxey Bay
St John's
Greeba
T.T. Course
Baldwin
Baldrine
Clay Head
Glen Maye
Crosby
Glen Vine
Onchan
Niarbyl
Dalby
FOXDALE
Union Mills
Onchan Head
Niarbyl Bay
483m
South Barrule
Braaid
DOUGLAS
Douglas Bay
Douglas Head
St Mark's
Newtown
Grenaby
Fleshwick Bay
Ballakilpheric
Isle of Man Steam Railway
Colby
Ballabeg
Santon
Bradda Head
Santon Head
PORT ERIN
Ballasalla
Ronaldsway Airport
Cregneish
CASTLETOWN
PORT ST MARY
Derbyhaven
Calf Sound
Calf of Man
Spanish Head
Scarlett Point
Castletown Bay
Langness Peninsula
Caigher Point
Dreswick Point
KEY TO THE WALKS
WALK 1 PEEL TO PORT ERIN
WALK 2 PORT ERIN TO PORT ST MARY
WALK 3 PORT ST MARY TO DOUGLAS
WALK 4 DOUGLAS TO LAXEY
WALK 5 LAXEY TO RAMSEY
WALK 6 RAMSEY TO BALLAUGH
WALK 7 BALLAUGH TO PEEL
WALK 8 FOXDALE LINE
WALK 9 THE HERITAGE TRAIL
WALK 10 THE MILLENNIUM WAY

Glen Maye

assumed that the visitor is staying in Douglas but it is easy to link to other resorts or to use private transport at least to the start of the walks. Each walk contains a number of options for half day walks or even shorter and these are described where appropriate.

Then follow two walks along disused railway lines and the final walk over the Millennium Way.

Walk 1

Peel to Port Erin(seven hours/13 miles)

Take public transport to Peel and leave it at the House of Manannan from where the walk starts. There are options to take two half day walks, one from Peel to Glenmaye and return and the other from Port Erin around Bradda.

Start by walking alongside the harbour to the bridge at the head of the harbour.

The site of the former railway station is now occupied by the House of Manannan which is operated by Manx National Heritage as part of *The Story of Mann*.

Cross the bridge at the head of the harbour and head towards the castle but after a short distance follow the broad track up the hill, being careful to take the grassy track sharp left at the corner as the castle comes into view. You will soon see that there are two distinct parts to the hill that dominates Peel. The first which you have just passed is Peel Hill and the next part is Corrin's Hill surmounted by Corrin's Tower.

From the saddle between the two hills you can if you wish carry straight on to the summit of Corrin's Hill; or choose to take the path to the right that follows the old horse tramroad to the quarry on the back of Corrin's Hill. The latter is by far the more spectacular but the path is close to the cliff edge in places so care is needed particularly with young children and this is so for many places on the walk.

Whichever way you have chosen you will end up at the same spot overlooking the south west coast of the Island. Niarbyl (literally meaning ' the tail' - from the tail of rocks stretching out to sea) is clearly seen. Cronk ny Irree Laa (hill of the dawn) dominates the skyline above with the hills stretching south to Fleshwick (green creek) and Bradda, with the Calf of Man just appearing in the far distance.

The path now becomes a real cliff path but it is easy to follow as it skirts the various bays and inlets. Look for Traie Cabbag (cabbage shore - so named after the wild cabbage that grows there) and the unusual rock known as the Bonnet Rock which is surrounded by water at most states of the tide. You will see why it has this local name when you find it.

Now as you approach Glen Maye (yellow glen) you have another choice. The path has to revert to the coast road here for a short distance. You can follow the path down to the mouth of the glen as you round the headland and take the path up the opposite side of the glen to join the main road. Alternatively carry on down into the glen and follow the lower path stopping to admire the waterfall before climbing the steps to the main road.

There is an opportunity here to break for lunch at Glen Maye before returning by public transport or walking back to Peel along the main road.

Turn right and follow the road down the hill and climb the other side to continue south parallel to and in sight of the coast all the way to Dalby (glen farm). Follow the signs through the village and start to climb and after a short distance look for the footpath signs directing you down the Dalby Laag Road. The narrow road parallels the coast, drops down to a pond and finishes. You must look for the signs again here and follow them crossing the pond on large stepping stones. Continue towards the large house looking for the signs and the stile directing you over the hedge and into the field opposite.

Follow the waymarkers and you will soon start to climb to a broad path on Manx National Heritage property that will take you south above Feustal (precipice) towards Cronk ny Irrey Laa. Cross the stone wall over the wooden stile. The path is on the top of a cliff and should be treated with extreme care. Above Gob ny Ushtey (headland of the waterfall - although the literal translation means beak of the water. The Manx often described headlands as looking like the bill or beak of a bird and so the description came into common use describing headlands) the path swings inland to cross a stream and wall. Now strike uphill past the old farmhouse at Eary Cushlin (Cosnahan's shieling), now a venture centre. Continue uphill following the signs all the way to the top of Cronk ny Irrey Laa. There are quite spectacular views all the way up the climb and when you reach the summit you will be at the highest point on the coastal path. Take time out to admire the view back over Niarbyl towards Peel with Corrin's Tower visible in the distance.

Now make your way down towards the Sloc (or Slough meaning pit or hollow) over open moorland. You will often find flocks of chough frequenting this area and they are quite a distinctive bird with their bright red beaks and legs contrasting with their black plumage. They are now quite rare in the British Isles and the Island is one of their last refuges.

At the Sloc you will leave the moorland and join the road very briefly. Almost immediately you must enter back on to the moorland again by the picnic site on the other side of the boundary wall. Here as so often with the coastal path you are faced with a choice. The easy wide track to the left or the path to the right which is for the more experienced walker and will take you to the summit of Lhiattee ny Bienee (literally meaning - summit on the side) commanding excellent views back towards Cronk ny Irrey Laa and the big bay below.

Take the wide track and follow it to Surby (a Norse word Saurbyr meaning moorland farm) where it joins a surfaced road. At Surby turn right and follow the road to Fleshwick (green creek) down the east side of the valley. As you approach the end of the valley look for the signs on the left of the road just after the farm which will take you over a stile to start a really steep climb that will take you to the top of Bradda.

This is where the alternative short walk from Port Erin joins the walk.

Take your time climbing the path and admire the views behind you all the way up the coast to Niarbyl and across the valley at Fleshwick. Once over the top of this climb the view opens out in front of you down the coast to the Sound. The descent into Port Erin is easy and you will pass Milner's Tower on your way to Port Erin here again you are faced with a number of alternative paths. Take the one following the coast through Bradda Glen and on to the upper Promenade at Port Erin. Walk into the village and follow the signs to the railway station and bus depot from where you will have a choice of transport back to Douglas.

For the short walk based on Port Erin we shall start from the railway station and cross the road into Bridson Street past the Cherry Orchard Hotel. Turn right into Bay View Road and left up Harrison Street and onto a Public Right of Way which will take you across the Rowany Golf Course. Be aware of golfers and keep an eye out for wayward golf balls! The path is clearly marked and the views are good. Keep heading for the valley ahead avoiding the junctions with other paths and eventually emerge at Honna Hill crossing through an old stone built stile in the boundary wall. Turn left and head up the hill to the top and look for the sign marking the Ernie Broadbent Walk off to the right. Follow this narrow road down the west side of the Fleshwick valley until joining the surfaced road to Fleshwick Beach just past the farm. We turn left and look for the signs showing where the Raad ny Foillan leaves the road a little distance further on and where we join the longer walk from Peel.

On this shorter walk there is time to walk down to the beach at Fleshwick and admire the views up the coast towards Niarbyl from sea level. The cliffs below the Carnanes sloping down to the sea are dramatic from here and we can see where the high level path from the Sloc descends to Fleshwick and why it is for the more experienced walker.

Port Erin

Walk 2

Port Erin to Port St Mary (Six miles/four hours)

This is perhaps the most beautiful of all the Island walks whatever the time of year and whatever the weather. You should allow about four hours in order to take time to admire the views.

It is possible to make your way back to Port Erin if you so wish along the road from the Sound via Cregneash Village which is also part of the Story of Mann and then by way of the Darragh Road (place where oak trees grow) from Cregneash into Port Erin

Having arrived in Port Erin make your way from Station Road down to the lower Promenade and follow the sweep of the bay to the Marine Biological Station. You will have to look very carefully for the start of the next section of the coastal path as it has a very inauspicious start from behind an electrical sub station!

Once you have found it, the path is easy to follow. There is a fairly stiff climb around the back of the Marine Biological Station and up above Kione ny Garee (literally meaning the end of the thicket) where fulmars nest on the north facing shaded cliffs throughout the year. The path levels out above Bay Fine and you will have a good view back towards Port Erin and Bradda Head before descending towards Aldrick (old people's creek). On the way you should look

Cregneash

out for an unusual finger of rock known as Jacob's Rock. Ahead is the Calf of Man and the Sound with Kitterland and Thousla Rock. You will often see the tide race here and if it is at all stormy you will be treated to some spectacular sea views.

Crossing National Heritage land the path skirts around Burroo Ned (nest hill) and you will see the back of Spanish head above Baie ny Breechyn (bay of the breeches - so named because it resembles a pair of blue trousers laid out on the sea). Pass through a gate and cross a small stream to commence the very steep assault on the back of the Cronk Mooar (big hill - although it has a local name of Cronk y Feeagh meaning hill of the raven, which is more appropriate as ravens do nest here). This is the southernmost hill in the Island. Not very high but you will know it is a hill after you have made the climb. Pause at the top and take in the views all round over the Sound and the Calf Island itself. If you are lucky and the wind is in the right direction you may hear the baying of the common seals as they bask on the rocks known as the Cletts (rocks) on the Calf Island immediately opposite this point.

The path now starts to drop still skirting the cliff edge and then turns north to start its run up the east coast. The path is very close to the edge above Black Head and care should be taken, particularly with children.

The path now starts to fall quickly towards Bay Stakka (a corruption of Baie yn Stackey referring to the stack of Sugar Loaf Rock) which it skirts and then climbs to the Chasms which are on the right. Again the path is exposed at this point and care should be taken before crossing the wall on a substantial stile heading towards the derelict building that was formerly a café.

Go through the wooden gate and follow the waymarked route alongside the wall on your left. This should avoid having to cross any of the Chasms which are deep clefts in the rock and quite an unusual phenomenon. Be careful to descend the path beside the wall on your left all the way to a metal kissing gate above Cashtal Kione ny Goagyn (meaning the castle of chasms head) or Sugar Loaf Rock as it is more popularly known because of its unusual shape. It is inhabited by colonies of guillemots, kittiwakes and fulmars with the occasional razorbill and sometimes puffins and this is perhaps the most spectacular view of the rock providing you have a good head for heights.

The path crosses the next field diagonally heading for a gap in the stone wall opposite. Before leaving the cliff edge you can just catch a glimpse of 'the anvil' or as it is sometimes called 'the pulpit rock' which is a rock standing clear of the cliff in the small bay behind the Sugar Loaf Rock.

Follow the well-defined path between walls eventually leading onto a surfaced road to Glenchass (an English corruption of Glion Shast meaning sedge glen) and Port St Mary.

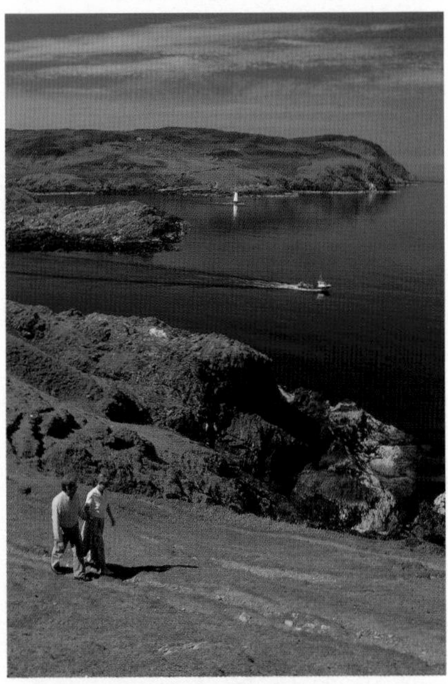

Looking out towards the Calf of Man

Port St Mary

At Glenchass the road forks. Take the right fork and follow the road downhill for a short distance looking for a sign on the right to take you to the shoreline at Perwick (harbour creek). The route follows the beach at Perwick and Traie Coon (narrow beach) before swinging up a zig zag path from the stony shoreline to join the path beside the Golf Course and on to Port St Mary Promenade. Walk along the sea wall passing the disused limekiln past the breakwater into Lime street and the inner harbour. Port St. Mary remains largely unspoilt but is now occupied by pleasure craft rather than commercial fishing boats.

Turn left at the end of Lime Street and then right to follow the lower promenade and join the Cain Karran elevated walkway which gives an impressive entrance into Chapel Bay which is without doubt one of the Islands prettiest and most sheltered bays. Walk up into the village where there is a choice of places to eat and from where it is possible to catch a bus back to Douglas.

Walk 3

Port St Mary to Douglas (eight hours)

Start this walk by taking public transport to Port St Mary and if by bus get off at the harbour or if by train there is a short walk from the station to the village.

The path continues around the Lower Promenade and Gansey Point to Bay ny Carrickey (bay of the rock) following the coast road to Fishers Hill for approximately one mile. You will pass the gatehouses and boundary wall to Kentraugh House and may just catch a glimpse of this fine mansion where there is a break in the windswept trees that form the boundary.

Continue along the sea wall and take the right fork at the bottom of the hill to follow the single track surfaced road almost on the shore line to Poolyvaaish (Poyll vaaish literally meaning the pool of death. The origin of the name is obscure but one likely explanation is that a slaughter house associated with the farm may have drained into one of the many sea pools). The whole area teems with birdlife and you should particularly look for herons which patiently fish in the rock pools and on the edge of the water competing with the curlew and the oyster catchers. The path continues through the farm buildings at Pooylvaaish and round the low headland beside the quarry from which the black limestone for the steps of St.Pauls Cathedral in London was obtained. Cross the stone stile over the wall to open onto the grassy headland at Scarlett (cormorant's cleft).

The path follows the edge of the fields skirting the rocks which change dramatically showing their volcanic origin and culminating in the stack known as Scarlett which is a volcanic plug to a vent long since extinct. The broken jagged rocks are the remains of an ancient volcanic lava flow. The rock changes from basalt to limestone as you approach Castletown the ancient capital of the Island dominated by its magnificent castle.

Enter the town square and turn right to skirt the castle passing the police station and immediately turning right again then left over the footbridge to cross the harbour. Turn right into Douglas Street and past the Nautical Museum which together with the castle is also part of the Story of Mann both of which have interesting presentations.

Continue along Douglas Street and right into College Green then follow the promenade towards King William's College and the airport. Carry on as far as Derbyhaven turning left along the shoreline as far as you can go. At the end look for the waymarkers which will take you around the edge of the airport boundary and under the approach lights gantry. You will climb onto an ancient raised beach which you must follow to Cass ny Hawin (the foot of the river) where the Santon river joins the sea through a dramatic gorge. The gorge was cut by the melt water from the retreating ice sheet during the ice age. You will have a commanding view of the gorge from the site of an ancient Bronze Age fort.

The path now follows the gorge inland until you come to a bridge crossing the river and then returns to the coast down the other side of the gorge. Although signposted it is often wet and difficult under foot in which case it may be best to take to the fields and follow the top of the gorge until you join the coast again.

Once at the coast the path is easy to follow along the top of the cliffs. You will be rewarded with good views all the way to Douglas. The next bay you will come to is Port Soldrick (sunny creek). Just where the path turns inland to drop down to the shoreline you will see some large caves in the opposite headland with a view of the coast north towards Santon Head. After travelling along the beach for a short distance climb back onto the path and you will quickly gain height to continue along the cliff top.

The next inlet is Port Grenaugh and again after reaching the shoreline climb up the other side of the bay. Look for the promontory fort and Viking settlement at Cronk ny Merrui (literally the hill of the dead people) on the right as you climb. Continuing along the coast you will pass Purt Veg (little port) and Santon Head before starting the climb up to Ballnahowe where the path goes inland once again.

The single track road crosses the steam railway before joining the Old Castletown Road. Turning right follow the road for little over a mile - take care as there is no footway. Descending Crogga hill (from the Norse Króká meaning winding river) you will pass Crogga House and its decorative lake before seeing a waymarker which will direct you down towards Port Soderick (has the same meaning as Soldrick - sunny or south facing creek) passing under the steam railway this time.

Keep to the road and take the left fork along the Marine Drive that you will now follow along the coast passing the inlet at Keristal. The coastal path follows the route of the former Marine Drive tramway all the way to Douglas. Note the change again in the rock formations with the contorted strata now in fragmented slate clearly visible in the cliffs all around you. Problems with the cliff faces have meant that the road is closed to through traffic but cars are able to use most of it so be aware. Approaching the old toll gate house means that you are almost at Douglas and as you round the corner there is the whole of the bay spread out before you.

The coastal path now descends the steps between the lighthouse and the Camera Obscura down to the breakwater and past the Lifeboat House. The Douglas Lifeboat is appropriately named Sir William Hillary after the founder of the Royal National Lifeboat Institution who lived in Douglas in the early part of the nineteenth century.

Walk 4

Douglas to Laxey (Nine miles/four hours)

This is a good half day walk with Laxey as its destination where there is a fine choice of places to have lunch and spend the afternoon in the Laxey Wheel area taking a look at the Island's rich industrial past.

Starting at the sea terminal on the Loch Promenade walk along the Loch Promenade walkway which was built in the 1870's to enclose part of the foreshore and extend the lower part of Douglas. Some of the original Victorian facade is now giving way to modern development and illustrates dramatically the changing face of Douglas. It is still possible to get a flavour of the grand Victorian facade of the promenade as we make our way north.

Stop opposite the Sefton Hotel to admire its elevation and that of the Gaiety Theatre. The church to the left and set back off the promenade was completed in 1849 and dedicated to St Thomas, the patron Saint of Architecture. It was designed by Ewan Christian R.I.B.A. an architect of Manx descent who was Architect to the Church Commissioners (1814 - 1895) and noted particularly for his work at Carlisle Cathedral. The building work was undertaken by local contractor Richard Cowle. It was built to serve the needs of an expanding town and the arrival of the tourist development along Loch Promenade led to it being referred to as 'the visitor's church'.

A fire in the tower in 1912 destroyed the bells and the organ that had been built and installed in 1886 by William Hill of London. The fire damage was repaired and a new peal of bells was installed five months later. At the same time the organ was repaired and enlarged and recitals and concerts are a regular feature of church life.

Continuing to the end of the promenade and more signs of redevelopment we approach the terminus of the unique Douglas Bay Horse Tramway which dates from 1876. It also adjoins the terminus of the Electric Tramway which runs between Douglas and Ramsey which commenced operation in 1895. Both tramways still operate and utilise original equipment making them a Mecca for transport enthusiasts the world over.

Continue past Port Jack and around the loop of Seaview Road admiring the coastal views which now appear with the houses overlooking Douglas Bay. Joining the Coast Road again look for the waymarker that will direct you along the cliff top almost through the front gardens of those houses before joining the road again at Lag Birragh (literally the sharp pointed hollow - referring to the rocks below). The path continues along King Edward Road to Groudle (narrow glen) where you should follow the narrow road down to the shore by the holiday homes. Cross the river by the footbridge and climb up the path to cross the Groudle Glen Railway. The railway, which was a Victorian novelty, is now restored and operated by enthusiasts throughout the summer months.

Follow the path upwards and on to a narrow surfaced single track road looking for a waymarker to direct you across the fields to Garwick. On the way look for the signpost to Lonan Old Church and take time to make a detour to see it and the standing Celtic Wheel Cross in the grounds.

Walk through the fields until the path joins Clay Head Road which you must follow towards Baldrine. Keep a look out for the waymarker directing you to Garwick and follow the fisherman's path to the shore and then immediately go all the way back up the other side of the glen following the signs to join the main road again.

Turn right at the top and continue towards Laxey, no pavement again so be careful, following the tramway. At Fairy Cottage there is an option if you know the state of the tide! At low water you can take another fisherman's path down onto the beach and walk to Laxey harbour which gives a lovely entry into Laxey. Otherwise you must continue down Old Laxey Hill into Old Laxey and the harbour.

Follow Glen Road to Laxey Village and up the hill under the church to the centre of the village. Christ Church Laxey is situated in what must be a unique setting for any church and its history is entwined with the mining history of Laxey. The village was a very busy place in the mid 1800's as a direct result of the mining industry. The population had increased significantly and with the temptation of public houses on the doorstep the need for a place of worship within the village was long overdue.

It is not surprising that we find that the Laxey Mining Company and one of its principal shareholders G.W.Dumbell was instrumental in promoting a church for the village. Part of the garden of the Mines Captains House was made available for the church to be built right in the middle of the village. The church was designed by Ewan Christian (whose name has already been mentioned) and built largely by the miners themselves.

Take a little time to enjoy this small church built in the early English style with its interesting scissorbeam roof and simple internal decor before lunching in Laxey followed by a walk up to The Laxey Wheel and the mines experience operated also by Manx National Heritage.

Return to the tram station and take a tram back to Douglas to complete a walk with a difference.

Laxey

Walk 5

Laxey to Ramsey (12 miles/six hours)

This walk starts from Laxey tram station in the heart of Laxey Village convenient to either bus or tram from Douglas.

Leave the station by the path alongside the station building and walk down to Captains Hill turning right to join Glen Road opposite St. George's Woollen Mills and make your way to the harbour. Look for the large factory type building on the opposite side of the river. This was built as the power generating station for the Laxey section of the Manx Electric Railway.

At the junction by the harbour bridge look to the opposite side of the road for the waymarker for the coastal path which you will follow up an old packhorse road to Ballaragh (of doubtful origin best seen as derived from Balley arraght meaning farm of the spectre or apparition). Continue up through Ballaragh to the top of the hill where views open towards Maughold Head and across the Irish Sea to Cumbria and the Lake District.

Manx Postbox

Maughold

The road curves away from the coast, but look for the waymarker on the corner that will take you over the fence and diagonally down through the fields. Cross the road and the tram track and continue on the footpath until it joins the Dhoon Glen Loop Road. Cross one stile on to the road and then immediately back over the adjacent stile to follow the track down to sea level again. It is worth the effort even though this is another of those down and back up again detours.

The path skirts the Dhoon Glen and you will catch a glimpse of the wheel case of the Dhoon Rhennie Mine (Dhoon is derived probably from an Irish word meaning fort and rhenny is a ferny place) which operated to extract lead and zinc but was not productive and was eventually abandoned. Then the mouth of the glen opens up and you will have a view of the headland of Kion e Hennin (Kione ny eaynin headland of the

Laxey Wheel

cliff. Kione literally means beak or bill of a bird but by common usage has come to mean headland) with it's inclined grey slate which is the native rock of the area. Immediately behind this headland there was a granite boss which for years was quarried for its pink Granite.

The path drops to the shore and then returns behind the picnic table. Follow the path within the glen climbing past the Island's most spectacular waterfall, which is made up of three falls which empty into a pool beside the path. A further steep climb will take you back to the point where you began this detour.

Turn right back onto the Dhoon Loop Road and follow it over the tramway back to the main road and turn right. Almost immediately turn right again and at the bottom of the hill turn right yet again making sure to take the right fork by the ford following the single track road down to Cornah (an ancient treen - land division-name).

You are now back at sea level again, but this time with a difference. Behind the shingle bank is a saltmarsh with an attendant variety of birdlife. The path crosses the river and follows an unsurfaced road known as Benussi's lane all the way up the right hand side of the valley heading inland. Cross the tramway again and the main road to continue up the Raad ny Quakerin (the Quaker's road) pausing to look at the Quakers burial ground at the summit.

Descending through Ballajora (farm of the strangers) there is a view of Maughold Head and the lighthouse. At the bottom of the hill look for the signs taking you right to Port Mooar (the great harbour). Follow the path round the coast through the tall grass to Gob ny Rona (headland of the seals) where you may very well see some seals. At Dhyrnane you will pass some derelict workings from an iron ore mine before climbing away from the shore. Cross some fields past a lime kiln to join the road to the lighthouse turning right for a short distance before turning left onto Maughold Brooghs. Follow the path over the headland through more old mine workings at Gob Ago (literally edge headland) before joining the road again and turning right towards Ramsey.

As before you have so many choices. You may carry on into Ramsey along the main road but again if the tide is out why not go down the slip at Port e Vullen (harbour of the mill) onto the shore and follow the cliff path around the headland at Tableland to rejoin the road again a little further on.

Either way it is back up to the main road passing Belle Vue tram stop to follow the main road again all the way down to Ramsey. At Ballure (Balley euar meaning yew tree estate or farm) you could make a detour into Ballure Glen and to Ramsey along the beach, but this latter option is only available at low water. Either way make your way into Ramsey along the promenade and the harbour.

The church of St. Maughold and Our Lady Star of the Sea at the end of the promenade was built in 1900 and designed by Giles Gilbert Scott.

Return to Douglas either by tram or bus from the tram station in Waterloo Road.

Walk 6

Ramsey to Ballaugh (18 miles/eight hours)

This walk is also part of the coastal footpath and is by way of a complete contrast embracing the northern alluvial plain.

The walk is very dependent on tidal conditions and should not be undertaken when the tide is rising. The ideal start is shortly after high water although there are alternatives which avoid the risk areas.

Starting from the tram station which is also close to the bus station make your way

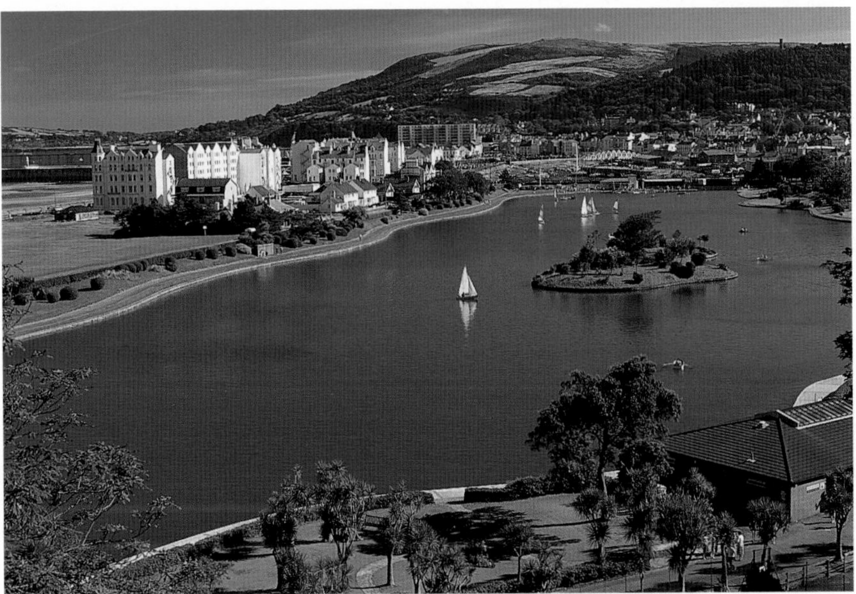

Mooragh Park

to the harbour and follow the quayside to the stone arched bridge at the head of the harbour. Cross over the bridge, turn right into North Shore Road to the Mooragh Promenade (Mooragh meaning waste land by the sea) and then left following the promenade as far as the Vollan. Here is where the first choice has to be made which is entirely dependent on the tide. If the tide is out then it is possible to walk all the way to the Point Of Ayre on the shingle beach. If not then there is no alternative other than to walk up the hill turn right and follow the road to Bride Village and onward to the Point of Ayre.

Now the geology of the cliffs has changed once more and they are all sand. The high cliffs at Shelag (here the original Norse name means seal creek or bay) are quite dramatic but because of erosion the bay no longer exists. The whole area continues to be subject to storm erosion as you will clearly see as you continue along the shore. If you have had to take the road to Bride and onwards then you will pick up the coastal path again at the Phurt (port). From the Phurt follow the raised beach which clearly illustrates the glacial formation of the northern plain. The whole of the Ayres was formed by alluvial deposit and here the terrain changes yet again with shingle under foot all the way around the northernmost tip of the Island.

The lighthouse, which marks the northernmost tip of the Island, was designed by Robert Stevenson and built by the Commissioners of Northern Lights in 1818. The shingle is constantly on the move as can be seen by the smaller lighthouse that was added 72 two years after the original. Like all the lighthouses around the coast of the British Isles it is no longer manned but is controlled from a remote central station.

Continue round the coast on the shore line, which is heavy going underfoot but worth it for the wild natural beauty to seaward, with bird life in abundance. Look for gannets with their spectacular diving and their vivid white that sets them apart from all the other birds. Curious seals often follow walkers as you make your way along the beach, you will also be constantly leapfrogged by flocks of oyster catchers.

Passing Rue Point and Blue Point where the rifle range and the old Coastguard lookout are located you will be back into sand. The whole of the northern plain has been drained by successive generations to bring back into use many acres of fertile agricultural land. The last major undertaking was the formation of a lengthy drainage channel which discharges at the Lhen (Lhen Mooar - meaning great ditch). You will know when you reach there as the Lhen Trench discharges across the shore and wading is the only way to get across so its boots off and round the neck.

Approaching Jurby Head the sand cliffs are back with a vengeance and continue almost to Peel. At Jurby Head, if the tide is well out, look for the remains of the trawler Passages which was driven ashore in 1929 in a north west gale becoming a total loss, the crew being successfully rescued by the rocket brigade of the day.

After passing Jurby Head we approach the Killane (from the Scandinavian kjarrland meaning brushwood land) where another drainage ditch discharges to the sea. Look for the signs shortly after here where the Ballaugh shore road joins the shoreline at the Cronk.

Leave the shore and walk to Ballaugh Village passing the old parish Church of St Mary de Ballaugh dating from the middle of the eighteenth century. It is noted for its leaning gate pillars which by reference to photographs and old guides must have been like that for a hundred years at least.

Walking towards Ballaugh you can admire the backdrop of the western hills and see the tower of the new Parish Church which we pass as we enter the village. Work on building the church commenced in May 1830. Many of the older parish churches were all located more or less centrally in the various parishes. As communities developed in the villages these churches were often too far from the people they were supposed to serve. Ballaugh was no exception although the old church was also considered too small as well too far from the centre of population; even though it was no more than a mile away near the coast.

The church, designed by Hanson and Welch, is built in local stone in a style unique amongst Island churches. The tall lancet type windows and intervening buttresses to the nave and the ornate pinnacles make it quite distinctive.

You will arrive in the centre of the village opposite the public house and beside the world famous Ballaugh Bridge very much part of the T.T. course. Return to Douglas or Ramsey by public transport.

Walk 7

Ballaugh to Peel (13 miles/five hours)

This walk is all easy going. Take public transport to Ballaugh and start the walk from the centre of the village.

Leave the village by Station Road and walk to the Cronk passing the two churches described in walk No.6. On the way you will pass the Dollagh and again as in all Manx place names there is more to the name than meets the eye. Much of the northern plain in early times was flooded and the land was covered with several large lakes. There are no visible signs of these lakes left now except in times of heavy rainfall when remnants appear here and there. Dollagh is a corruption of Doufloch (black lake) other places like Ellan Rhenny (ferny island) and Ellan Bane (white island) and even the parish name of Ballaugh (a corruption of Balley ny Loughey - lake farm) gives a clue to what this area was like in early times.

Jurby Head

At the Cronk turn left and follow the Bollyn (Boayl ein - spot of the birds) Road as far as the Orrisdale Road. There are good views of the western hills which form the backdrop to Bishopscourt, the ancient seat of the Bishop of Sodor and Mann but now a private residence. Turn right at the junction with the Orrisdale Road and follow the road through Orrisdale (from the Scandinavian Orrastaðr meaning estate of the moorfowl) look for the signpost at the corner after the farm, which leads to the shore at Glen Trunk. Go through the gate and follow the wide grassy track to the shore passing one of the best preserved lime kilns on the Island.

Once on the shore you will be able to see Peel in the distance so turn left and walk along the shore flanked by steep sand cliffs and you will see that these are also subject to erosion - for that reason it is not advisable to walk close underneath them. You will notice here that in addition to the oyster catchers, herring gulls and black backed gulls you will be accompanied by flocks of curlew which graze the foreshore and live on the hill slopes of the western hills. Ringed plover are often seen in this area and the occasional chough.

As you approach Glen Wyllin (glen of the mill) you will see some sea defence works on the foreshore in an attempt to slow down the rate of erosion. You will pass these and a short distance further along the shoreline look for the waymarkers directing you off the shore at Glen Mooar (the great glen).

Leave the shore here and make your way up the narrow surfaced road to the main coast road. Look across the road and you will see a waymarker directing you into the glen. Follow the path as far as the stone pier which is one of two piers that carried the railway across the glen on lattice steel girders. Climb the roughly cut steps up the side of the embankment to join the disused railway track that now forms part of the coastal path for the next three miles as far as the old station at St. Germain's Halt.

Look back from the elevated position once on the track and you will immediately get an impression of just how severe the erosion of the sand cliffs is at this point. In places it will not be long before the coast road will be threatened. There are a couple of farm crossings before we approach a rock cutting and the road overbridge at Skerisdale (or more correctly Skeresstaõr from the Norse meaning rocky farm). The railway now runs closer to the sea than the road and you can imagine just how dramatic the journey by train was as it clung to the cliffs and spanned the glens on viaducts and embankments.

Leaving the cutting the trackbed emerges onto one of those embankments as it spans Glion Cam (the winding glen) and opens up views of Peel and the Castle on St. Patrick's Isle in the distance. The coast road can be seen to the left and above as it winds its way around the head of the glen giving it the local name of the Devil's Elbow.

After a further half mile in a shallow cutting, which is sometimes quite wet and muddy, the path emerges into the open and now really does cling to the cliff. When the railway was still operating, this section known as the 'donkey bank', gave continuous problems with settlement that you will be able to see as you walk along. Below you can also see that rocks are back on the shore line at Gob y Deigan as you cross the second of the embankments. From here on the physical features of the coast change yet again from the sand cliffs to slate and then to red sandstone as we get nearer to Peel.

The path continues on the trackbed for a further mile crossing yet another glen on an embankment at Glion Booigh (the dirty glen). It is worth stopping on the embankment to look down at the trees growing in this glen. There is a great variety with some surprises and in many ways it is one of the unspoilt corners of the Island and only really appreciated from this location. The path now curves left to join the coast road at the site of the former St. Germain's Halt with the old station building and gatehouse still just recognisable for what they were.

Leave the track here and follow the road for a short distance downhill and round the corner at the bottom. Look for the waymarker on the right after the corner and go through the kissing gate to join the headland path. The path climbs some rough cut steps and reaches a promontory above Cass Struan (stream end). Stop and look north back along the route that we have just walked and you will see the sand cliffs stretching all the way north to the prominent white outline of Jurby Church and Jurby Head in the distance. Now look down below where you are standing and you will see the sandstone to which I referred which outcrops here in a glorious burst of russet red.

The path now continues to Peel along the headland above Traie Fogog (or more correctly Traie Feoghaig - meaning periwinkle shore) commanding the best views over Peel and the Castle. Continue on the headland path and descend down into the town and the Promenade. There are several places to take refreshment and any of the roads off the promenade lead to the town centre and the bus station for return to Douglas.

These walks make up the Coastal Path and if you manage to walk all them you will have successfully completed the Raad ny Foillan.

Walk 8

The Foxdale Line (2.5 miles/one hour)

This short walk follows the disused railway line which connected the Foxdale lead mines to the rest of the Island's railway network at St Johns. The best option is to take a bus to Foxdale and start from the old station which is adjacent to the primary school.

The Foxdale Line was built in 1886 by the Foxdale Railway Company, an offshoot of the Manx Northern Railway as an opportunist venture to win lucrative mineral traffic from the Isle of Man Railway.

Prior to the building of the railway to Foxdale, all the ore was taken by horse and cart to St. Johns for onward transmission by the Isle of Man Railway to Douglas Station. It then had to be loaded again into horse drawn carts and taken to the harbour at Douglas. The contract for the carriage of the ore came up for renewal and the Manx Northern bid was successful.

With the Foxdale Railway completed and with access into the mines together with a direct line to Ramsey harbour over the Manx Northern Railway metals the contract was won. It was to become a financial burden to the Manx Northern leading to its eventual downfall. In the end everything came into the ownership of the Isle of Man Railway.

When mining came to Foxdale it brought with it a tremendous increase in population. Public houses sprang up in its wake and it soon supported a constable and a jail. Methodism found a strong footing in the area as in Laxey. The established church appointed a chaplain to Foxdale in 1850 but it was to be 1881 before Foxdale had its own church. Public subscription and a handsome donation from the mining company resulted in the foundation stone being laid in 1874 by Mrs Cecil Hall. The church, designed by James Cowle, was consecrated by Bishop Rowley Hill on Whitsun Tuesday,7th. June 1881 as a chapel of ease to Kirk Patrick Parish Church. The village became a parish district in its own right some years later. The church can be seen on the opposite side of the valley beyond the old school.

It is hard to imagine now what this area was like at the height of the mining boom with lead and silver being produced to an annual value of £50,000 at the time that the railway was built. There were 350 people employed in the mines. The three main shafts in Foxdale were Potts, Beckwiths and Bawdens. The deepest was Beckwiths, which reached a depth of 320 fathoms (1,920 feet) by 1902 and yet by 1911 the industry had declined and the Isle of Man Mining Co. had ceased working.

Starting by the old station building which is opposite the school in Mines Road our walk is all downhill at a steady gradient of 1 in 49. There is quite a wide defined track which runs from the road beside the school. This is the start of the track bed and the building on the left is the station building. There was a shallow platform with brick edging served by a single line with a run round loop. The area presently occupied by the school was the site of the principal spoil heap from Beckwiths mine. A temporary siding was built into this area in the 1930's to assist with the removal of this spoil which was mostly used in the construction of the playing fields which now form the basis of the National Sports Centre in Douglas (see the Heritage Trail walk). The spoil from Bawdens shaft formed a massive spoil heap behind the station which was hemmed in between these two mountains of waste. A scene very different from today and very difficult to imagine.

Beyond the station building there was a small brick structure supporting a water tank for the locomotives. A single line climbed behind the back of the station at a gradient of 1 in 12 to cross the road and enter the mines yard where the ore was loaded into the wagons for Ramsey via St.Johns. This line was always referred to as 'the back of the moon' an apt description if you had seen the area after the mines had ceased working. Before starting the walk just walk up Mines Road a short distance where the line crossed the road and you should should just be able to see the remnants of the crossing with the running rails and check rails in the road surface, the only visible remains of the Foxdale Railway.

Returning to the station you now start to walk down the line. While the first part near the school is somewhat changed you soon

Getting up Steam

come onto the old trackbed which is quite unmistakably railway as it skirts behind the miners cottages in Higher Foxdale. On the hillside to the right there are still some visible remains of the oldest mine in the area particularly near the river.

Now we are very close to the road and the line ran on a high stone built embankment before swinging left to cross the road on a steel girder skew bridge (Lukes Bridge) The road meanwhile prescribing a double corner as it dropped under the bridge to continue to Lower Foxdale (The name Foxdale is an anglicised corruption of Forsdalr a Scandinavian word meaning waterfall dale). The bridge was removed when the track was lifted in the early 1970ís. We must climb through the stile in the boundary wall and cross the road to the opposite side where there are steps leading up the old bridge abutment and back to the trackbed.

Now the formation can be really appreciated and we continue on an embankment towards Lower Foxdale with a view of Slieau Whallian ahead. We cross over the accommodation road to Ballamore farm (from an Irish family name - Moreís farm) on a small bridge. The line entered a cutting through rock as the line curves left and approaches Waterfall Halt which was the only intermediate stop on the line. At Waterfall little remains to show what was there. Originally planned to have a passing loop it was completed with only the single running line and a small wooden building on the flat area to the right.

We have to walk out of the station area on to the Ballanass road to by-pass the small bridge, now demolished, which carried the line over the Gleneedle stream a tributary of the Foxdale river. You will be able to see the abutments of this bridge from the road which we are only on for a very short distance before regaining the trackbed. The halt served the community of Lower Foxdale and also attracted visitors to the Hamilton Falls where the stream cascades down a rock face before joining the main river.

Back on the line we walk under the road overbridge carrying the Ballanass road over the railway (Balla n eas Manx Gaelic meaning farm of the waterfall). We are in a short cutting under trees and can probably hear the sound of the waterfall below us on the right. We emerge to curve around the hillside with lovely views towards the central valley dominated by Greeba Mountain. The line was built on an embankment and followed the natural lie of the land. There was an old mine on the left but nothing remains but a very overgrown spoil heap. The occasional telegraph pole reminds us of the railway.

We are now approaching Slieauwhallian farm (an obscure word which could refer to a personal name, possibly Mc Aleyn, or it could refer to hill of the whelps) and entering a wooded area. We pass under the bridge carrying an accommodation road associated with the farm and you will see that the construction was of a very simple nature and used concrete for the abutments. After the bridge the line passes through a very attractive section before curving left alongside the plantation which is part of the larger Slieauwhallian plantation. Not there of course when the railway was built.

Unfortunately you have to leave the line at the end of the plantation and veer off to the left and join the Slieauwhallian back road which we follow to the right downhill to the Patrick Road and right again to the next junction.

Before leaving the track bed it is worth looking where the track continued on an embankment which was almost forty feet high. Although now much overgrown it still gives an indication of the amount of material needed for its construction. The line curved to thent of material needed for its construction. The line curved to the right to cross the Foxdale river on two steel spans carried on a central stone pier between two abutments.

If you like you can turn right at the junction and walk a short distance towards the Hope and see where the line crossed the river after which it curved around in a left handed sweep to cross over the Peel Line and into St Johns. If you return to the junction with the Patrick Road you can carry on towards the village as far used as a car park which was the site of the St. Johns Station which was originally built by the Isle of Man Railway.

Walking further up Station Road cross over the Foxdale line just before the Post Office. You can look over the right hand parapet wall and see where the line came into St Johns behind Pretoria Terrace with the embankment climbing away towards Foxdale and over the Peel line. Looking over the left hand parapet you can clearly see the St Johns terminus of the Foxdale railway. The station was a grand building by comparison with that belonging to the Isle of Man Railway. It was similar in style to the station building at Foxdale. There was a passing loop at the station with goods sidings and the connection to the Manx Northern Railway beyond.

Finish the walk here and use public transport to go on to Peel or Douglas.

Walk 9

The Heritage Trail (11.5 miles/4 hours)

Make your way to the top of Douglas Harbour and into the Railway Station forecourt for the start of this easy walk.

When the railway was built in 1873 the Isle of Man Railway Co. had a simple wooden building as its station and its offices located in Athol Street which was then and still is to some extent the business centre of the town. Surprising then for such a small

Douglas

Island that by 1892 the railway company had risen in stature to build a station which would be the envy of many main line railways in the British Isles let alone comparable narrow gauge railways. The railway had arrived.

The Heritage Way follows the route of the first line to be completed which connected Douglas to Peel. Unfortunately the first half mile or so has been extensively built over so you have to make a detour before joining the line at the Quarterbridge.

Leave the station forecourt by the steps under the clock tower taking time to admire the grandeur of the station buildings and the grand entrance from Athol Street.

Make your way up Peel Road passing the shops on the left which were built by the ever enterprising Railway Co. Follow the road to the junction with Pulrose Road and turn left over the bridge. It is worth stopping to look at this bridge which was built in 1938 to replace an earlier level crossing. This is the route of the line we are following but we cannot yet join it. You will note that the bridge has two arches making provision for doubling the line, something that never happened. You will also be able to make out the route of the track bed as it threads its way behind the development of this area, which has taken place over the last 25 years.

Continue on towards the Power Station and turn right immediately before the bridge over the Douglas River and follow the pathway behind the Bowl, part of the King George V playing fields. The whole area was reclaimed using waste from the spoil heaps at the Foxdale mines. The Isle of Man Railway locomotive No.15 Caledonia was almost exclusively used to haul thousands of tons of material here between 1935 and 1939.

The path takes you to the confluence of the River Dhoo (black river) and the River Glass (green river) and now you can see how the name of the town of Douglas evolved. Follow the right fork alongside the Glass and cross it by the bridge which leads to the National Sports Centre. Continue following the river for a short distance past the rear of the grandstand and join the railway track behind the office building. This is where the railway crossed the river on a skew lattice girder bridge.

Now the walk can be started in earnest with a short walk on the old track bed until we reach the site of the level crossing which carried the railway across the Castletown Road. Note the crossing keepers gatehouse on the left. Take care crossing the road, visibility is restricted and it is a very busy road.

All of the disused railways have now been used as service corridors for gas, electricity, water and telephones. At the same time they became public rights of way and were gradually improved for walkers. In 1989 the Peel section which was the most complete was designated The Heritage Railway Trail. Work is still continuing on its improvement with the ultimate aim of making a cycle way to broaden its use.

The next section of the track bed has been made into a vehicular access road to the inside of the T.T. Course when the main road is closed for motorcycle racing. Continue behind Quarterbridge Lodge and climb the gate across the track and walk between the stone boundary walls. On the left you will see Kirby Estate and if you are lucky you may catch sight of grey herons which roost here and range the river. (The name Kirby is Scandinavian in origin and means Church Farm.)

Passing under the road you are approaching the site of the former Braddan Halt. This was used in connection with Open Air Sunday Services at Braddan Parish Church which you will shortly just be able to see to the left. It was not uncommon to see ten coach trains on this short special service from Douglas and hundreds of visitors getting off the train with no platform and walking up the steps by the bridge and up Vicarage Road to the fields behind the new parish church.

Leave the surfaced roadway and carry straight on along the old track bed now more recognisable as a disused railway. The River Dhoo which has never been very far away is now beside the railway. The local Commissioners have provided a wooden walkway between the railway and the river as part of a conservation scheme.

At Union Mills the line curves left after crossing the River on a steel girder bridge. This replaced an earlier stone built structure which gave rise to trouble with flooding in the early years of the railway. A small wayside halt existed here at the outset in connection with a horse racing course at the Strang.

Now with industry left behind the scenery becomes more pleasant. It is hard to realise that even as late as 1960 there was little or no industrial development between Pulrose Bridge and Union Mills!

Entering Union Mills Station through the tall trees which have grown with the railway we are now 2½ miles from Douglas. Early photographs show almost no cover at all. Successive station masters took a tremendous pride in the station which became noted for its wonderful rhododendron and floral displays.

The station was on the curve and had a very long passing loop which was added after 1906. On the left you will see the single platform serving the station. Look for the name of the manufacturer of the non slip paving slabs which form the edge of the platform. Also on the left before we reach the platform there is a roadway accessing the station area. There was a short trailing siding here serving a cattle dock and for goods traffic. The wooden station building was situated on the right just before the line passed under the road.

Part of the development of the Heritage Trail has been the inclusion of some picnic tables and also descriptive boards. Here at Union Mills a static display has been included. The Gibbins breakdown crane, one of two operated by the IMR, is displayed on a small section of track. Dating from 1893 it was hand operated and had a lifting capacity of 8 tons.

Immediately after crossing the River Dhoo yet again (the original steel structure was removed when the line was being dismantled) continue past a small industrial area where the remaining parts of the old Union Mills (the name evolved because a corn mill and a woollen mill built on the same site by William Kelly both drew water for their machinery from the same dam) can still be seen and still in use as small industrial units. The Mills were a big employer for this area in the early part of the nineteenth century.

Later they were owned by the Dalrymple family who continued to operate them until the end of the century. Dalrymple Maitland was a director of the railway and locomotive No11 was named after him.

Cross the Trollaby stream (possibly the stream of the trolls) and now enter open country as the line sweeps into the central valley of the Island. The River Dhoo is still on our left and you can see remnants of the curragh (bog) between the river and the railway. Much of the central valley was like this, with wet boggy land, water meadows and willow growing in what was in effect the flood plain of the river.

Henry Vignoles when he surveyed the route for the line chose a route which skirted the valley floor and just managed to keep above the water table. The line passes Glen Lough (literally Lake Glen) and then is straight for a short distance to cross the road at Closemooar (great enclosure), just after milepost 4. The crossing keepers gatehouse still survives and is on the left before the crossing.

There was a short cutting here and then the line ran straight towards Marown Church with Greeba Mountain dominating the view. The track bed here has also been surfaced to allow access to the nearby sewage works. Be careful of lorries accessing the works.

The trackbed passes behind the parish church and swings left entering more of the curragh land before approaching another road crossing which was controlled by a level crossing where once again the gatehouse still remains.

Cross the road and enter the playing fields. This was the site of Crosby Station some 4¾ miles from Douglas. Nothing remains to give a clue as to what was here. There was a passing loop and the facing point for this was positioned just before the level crossing and two tracks crossed the road. This meant that when trains passed here the road was obstructed for longer than usual. If the second train was late the gates would often be opened in between the passing operation. There was a typical I.M.R. wooden station building, painted green and

Plains of Heaven

cream, on the right just as we enter the playing fields. And just beyond that a wooden goods shed served by a siding off the passing loop with a further short siding to a cattle dock. The whole of which was partly screened by a wooden boarded fence.

Greeba (an obscure Scandinavian word meaning peak) is now much closer and the hills on both sides are closing in on the railway. You are still climbing and haven't yet reached the summit. On the hill on the left above the Highway Depot you can see the old school which served the Parish of Marown.

Leaving the playing fields you are soon back on the old trackbed. Straight ahead is Creg y Whallian (rock of the whelp) with Cooilingill Farm (low nook) on the hillside. You will just be able to see the edge of Archallagan Plantation to the left on the skyline. The River Dhoo has its source in the centre of the plantation before tumbling down the hill below Cooilingel and joining the Greeba River on our left.

The line swings right as it passes 5 miles with Greeba and Slieau Ruy (red mountain) straight ahead. You are now into the true remaining curragh of the central valley as you approach and cross the track leading to Cooilingel Farm. This crossing was an accommodation crossing and the gates were always open to the railway. Walk over another short bridge which crosses the Greeba river and continue close under Creg y Whallian. This is the narrowest part of the valley and very near to the summit of the line.

The next level crossing over the Rhenny road (boayl y rhennee - place of the fern) was also an accommodation crossing. The house with the unusual farm buildings on the right is Northop (another Scandinavian word meaning north village). Here is another chance to look at Greeba before the curragh closes in and we pass through a very wet area which was the site of an early settlement. You emerge approaching the Ballacurry Road which again was an un-manned crossing. The summit of the line at 185ft. was at the small stream after the Ballacurry Road. The Greeba Sports field is on our right just visible through the trees. (Ballacurry meaning marsh farm)

This is the site of an accident in 1909

when the locomotive No.2 Derby acting as pilot engine on a late train running to Peel had the misfortune to hit a fallen tree being completely derailed and falling onto its side. As you will see later this was the second accident to involve this locomotive.

Passing through Greeba the curragh is still visible in places but over the years drainage work and farming activity has reclaimed a large portion of it. The wooded hill ahead is Slieau Whallian although its true summit is further to our left. The hill dominates St. Johns and it is up the flank of that hill that the Foxdale Railway climbed at 1 in 49 to the mines at Foxdale. This is the point from where the Isle of Man Railway Co. proposed to build a line to Foxdale at one time and their branch would have made off to the left, climbing the side of the hill to the left above Kenna (Aodha's hill - Aodha being a personal name of Irish descent).

Cross the Kenna Road which was yet another un-manned accommodation crossing. After a shallow reverse curve under the trees the track runs straight all the way to St. Johns.

Now Slieau Whallian is much closer and you can see the gatehouse for the crossing keeper at the Curragh Road level crossing. The track bed has been surfaced here and an additional road built serving an amenity site. You cross the road and the stile onto the right hand track which is the original route of the railway and pass under the bridge which carried the Foxdale Railway over the Peel line. The bridge is covered with ivy, but you can see the brick arch springing from the stone abutments.

Now you are approaching the site of St. Johns station which grew from a very modest beginning to become the 'Crewe Junction' of the Island railways. In it's final form the line was single, passing under the bridge and running for a short distance parallel to a three lane carriage shed, steel framed and galvanised sheet clad, on the right. There was a fourth carriage siding in the open on the far side of the shed.

There was a small signalbox near the trees standing in the middle of the grassed area to our right. Here the line split into two each with a passing loop and served by a low single brick high platform in the centre of the two passing loops. This is where the Ramsey line and the Peel line split. There was a brick structure carrying a water tank at each end of the central platform. To the right there were sidings serving a cattle dock, the remains of which can still be seen, and also a head shunt to the carriage sidings.

St.Johns was served by a simple wooden station building which was situated on the left near the road the site having now been absorbed into housing development. It had a small waiting room ticket office and station master's office and this building was retained to the end despite the relative importance of the station.

Two lines crossed the road on a gated level crossing with the Peel line on the left and the Ramsey line on the right. To continue we have to make a slight detour from the original route of the line which cannot be followed alongside the Mart as the bridges have been removed. Cross the road and through the gate opposite leading to the sewage works and rejoin the track alongside the works.

Walking down from the road look at the interesting red brick building behind the hedge on your right. It was the terminus of the Foxdale Railway and was a grand building by comparison with the station belonging to the Isle of Man Railway. It was similar in style to the station building at Foxdale.

Passing through the gated stile you are back on clear trackbed again. The two lines were still running parallel with the Peel line on the left and the Ramsey line on the right. And you will see the Ramsey line start to rise alongside as you approach the two bridges crossing the River Neb at Ballaleece (Leece's farm). The difference in height between the two bridges shows how the Ramsey line was already gaining the height needed to cross the Peel road as it swings away to the right.

The Peel line meanwhile makes a gradual descent from the river crossing before levelling out on the flood plain of the Neb (the meaning of the name of the river is obscure). The river still meanders about this ancient flood plain and it has prescribed a loop around to the left towards the Patrick Road and joining with the Foxdale river since leaving the bridge at Ballaleece. Now it is back alongside the railway on the approach to Shenharra (meaning Old Ballaharra and may refer to an ancient earthwork).

The river starts another meander away to the left as you approach the cutting at Ballawyllin (Byllinge's farm) which was notorious in winter for collecting snow. The cutting is through the tail of what appears to be a moraine which was deposited at the time of the retreat of the ice sheet that covered the Isle of Man during the Ice Age.

Through the crossing at Ballawyllin and you can now see the true flood plain extending out towards Patrick and the full extent of Peel Hill and Corrins Hill, surmounted by Corrins tower. Further to the left are the Creggans (literally rocky place but describing the small rocky outcrop) forming the southern boundary to Knockaloe (Caley or Allowe's hill), the site of a First World War Internment Camp. A branch of the railway was built to serve this camp and you will see where it joined the Peel line shortly. The line ran straight for a short distance before skirting the sand cliffs of Ballatersen (part of the old Bishops Barony but literally meaning - farm of the crozier) now the location of the Peel Golf Course. You will notice that the railway passed through the last remnants of the Curragh and if you are particularly observant will see the remains of some of the drainage channels dug in the 1940's as a winter employment scheme in a further attempt to drain this area.

Now under the cliffs the track passed

Spring time near Crosby

through boggy ground again which gave the railway a great deal of trouble throughout its life. You can get some idea of the nature of the ground as we pass close under the sand cliffs. The willow catkins are a sight to behold in the spring and the area abounds with the yellow heads of the wild Iris.

A little further on and the river is back alongside the railway and slowed by a dam which was built for the Glenfaba Mill (as is so often the case with place names we find a mixture of English and Manx. It ought to be Myllin Glenfaba meaning - Mill in the glen of the Neb). The pond is known locally as the 'red dub', and you can see where the mill race was taken off the dam and under the track on its way to the mill. The name for the area, which also gives its name to the weir is the Congary (rabbit warren)

Before reaching the mill you will cross a small stream by means of a footbridge. Pay particular attention to the widening of the track bed just after the bridge. This is where the branch railway to Knockaloe Internment Camp left the Peel line by means of a trailing point from this direction. You can just make out the line of the branch as it curved round to cross the river on a wooden trestle bridge to climb for a little over a mile at a gradient of 1 in 20 to Patrick Village and Knockaloe.

Next on the right is the Glenfaba Mill and some indication of what it was like can be gleaned from the size and shape of the building. The water wheels remain and the overflow from them discharged under the track into the river. In fact the railway occupied the original river bed here and the river was re-aligned at the time of its building

The railway passed under the Patrick Road and alongside the river which was also diverted here to allow the railway to run through this natural gorge on a gentle curve. This was the scene of an earlier accident in 1874 when the ill fated locomotive No.2 Derby fell into the river when the original embankment gave way following heavy rain. It was the first train of the day and although the driver saw that the track had been washed away he was unable to stop. The driver and fireman both fell with the engine but were uninjured as was the only passenger who fortunately occupied one of the coaches that did not leave the track. The railway was temporarily diverted on a reverse curve to the right almost on the original line of the river whilst the present retaining wall was built on the original alignment.

Follow the railway through the remaining fields of Glenfaba farm as we enter Peel through the back door past the old power station on the left. The Total Oils storage depot and the new Peel Power station on the right are new additions. When the railway was running the first buildings encountered were the brick kilns of the Glenfaba Brick Co. with their tall chimneys. Brick built of course and dare I say aesthetically more pleasing than the slip form concrete chimney presently occupying the site.

Straight ahead and on the left hand side of the track is one of the original kipper houses now operated as a working museum and worth a visit. The modern kipper houses are in the fish yard on the right.

The railway finally arrived at Peel Station by a level crossing across Mill Road and onto the station site which had been reclaimed from the harbour bed. The water tank, the station building and goods shed are the only remains of the station itself, with the last two buildings incorporated into the House of Manannan which now occupies the site. Behind the water tank there was a small engine shed and on the right a cattle loading dock and the goods shed which had a loading bay into Mill Road which can still just be seen. The station ended with four roads and a run round loop served by a long platform after having undergone several changes throughout its life.

Now take a break at the Creek Hotel (originally The Railway Hotel) for some well-earned refreshment.

The Railway stopped running between Douglas and Peel in 1972 after five years of uncertainty. The rails had been lifted and sold for scrap before the Isle of Man Government stepped in and purchased everything which fortunately included the Port Erin line which remained intact although it had been a close call.

There is much to see in Peel which has retained much of its original character as well as The House of Manannan which is part of The Story of Mann.

Walk 10

The Millennium Way (26 miles – northern section 14 miles, southern section 12 miles)

This can be undertaken as a full day walk or as two walks with the break at Crosby.

The Millennium Way was the first long distance path to be introduced in the Isle of Man as part of the celebrations associated with 1000 years of independent government. Opened in Easter 1979 it was based on the ridgeway used by the Norse Kings from their ancient landing place on the Sulby river near Skyhill to travel to their fortress on the southern plain. The road is recorded in the Cronica Regum Mannie et Insularum (the Chronicles of the Kings of Man and the Isles) which was the first written record of events within the Island, kept by the monks of Rushen Abbey.

Take public transport either tram or bus to Ramsey and make your way from the tram station to the harbour which is a short distance along Parliament Street and down Post Office Lane opposite the Courthouse. Turn left at the harbour and follow it to the junction with Bowring Road. Note the shipyard on the opposite side of the harbour which was built on the site of a former salt works.

Cross the road at the top of the harbour and look for the public footpath sign leading to Pooyldhooie (pool of the black ford) where a nature reserve has been constructed on what used to be the town tip. It is now a very pleasant walk and a credit to the local commissioners and the volunteers who have carried out the work.

The path emerges by the Whitebridge which crosses the Sulby river and this must have been the most likely place for the Vikings to have made their safe harbour. At the time of their invasions and subsequent settlement the Island was a very different place and the Sulby river was by far the biggest river. Here they could sail their longships at least a mile and a half from the open sea and moor them in a sheltered lagoon, something which was not possible anywhere else on the Island.

The Vikings divided the Island, with settlements on the fertile northern plain and the southern plain. To travel between the two the Kings of Mann used the 'regiam viam' (the king's road) described in the Chronicles. It is the oldest record of any road in the Island and is the route that the Millennium Way generally follows.

Walk up Gardeners Lane to the main road and turn right for a short distance looking for the distinctive waymarkers for the Millennium Way striking off to the left over the bulk of Skyhill (the Norse named it Skógarfjall - the wooded hill). Follow the path up through the plantation which was the site of a battle in 1079 when Godred Crovan overcame the native Manx and assumed kingship of the Island.

On leaving the plantation the track opens out on the level near some rugged flat topped pine trees at Park ny Earkan (pasture of the lapwing). Stop and look back over the northern plain formed by the outwash from the retreating ice sheet which covered the Island during the ice age towards the Point of Ayre in the far distance.

Carry on to the top mountain gate and enter the open moorland. The track is still discernible and there are waymarkers which you will follow to a very wet boggy area. Cross by means of the planked walkway provided and be careful to follow the waymarkers off to the right heading for a cairn on the skyline in the saddle between Slieau Managh (mountain of the Monks) and Snaefell (snow mountain).

The 'regiam viam' veered off to the left here and follows the line of the mountain road for some distance travelling around the east flank of Snaefell. The Millennium Way favours the west flank to keep away from the traffic on the mountain road and at the same time introduce you to some of the more inaccessible places in the Island.

Pass the cairn and carry on over the saddle a short distance to join the mountain wall above Block Eary reservoir (from blakkärg meaning black shieling). Follow the mountain wall where it turns steeply down below the massive bulk of Snaefell. Cross the wall at the bottom by the stile and over the river.

The way strikes off steeply from the river and at right angles to it. It can be wet here at all times of the year but it is only for a short distance. As you climb it is worth looking back across the valley at the route you have just walked. You should just be able to make out the shape of some circular mounds. These are the shielings where the young men used to live with their animals on the mountain pasture during the summer months. Another remnant of a past way of life, and the best example of such structures on the Island.

Follow the waymarkers across the mountain until you pick up a stone wall and sod dyke which is part of a large earthwork known as Cleigh yn Arragh (stone rampart). Follow this until you reach a forestry department track and then the Tholt y Will Road.

Cross the road at the signpost and strike diagonally down the mountain side heading towards the mountain ahead which is Beinn y Phott (very loosely interpreted as turf peak). At the bottom of the valley cross the river by means of an old stone bridge which was built and used by the miners who operated the mine which is upstream a short distance. The stone structure that you can see is the remains of the wheelcase of the water wheel used in connection with the mine which was closed in 1867.

Climb up on the left hand bank of the gulley being careful at the top to take the left hand fork and head for the signpost which you should be able to see on the Brandywell Road.

This is where the Millennium Way joins the route of the old 'regiam viam' again. Cross the road and follow the track over the saddle between Beinn y Phott and Carraghyn (meaning scabby with reference to its stoney top) as far as the mountain gate which gives access to a rough track which you follow for almost two miles. The views open up over the Baldwins and on towards Douglas in the distance as you skirt the shoulder of Carraghyn.

The track starts to drop down at Cronk Keeil Abban (the hill of St.Abban's church) where an old keeil was located near an ancient Tynwald site which is on your right. At St. Lukes's Church, built as a chapel of ease to Kirk Braddan, join a surfaced road taking you downhill into West Baldwin.

At West Baldwin cross the bridge and the road to follow the signs up a track through Ballagrawe (Balla ny Groa farm of the cotes or coops) and across the fields of Ballalough (farm of the lakes). After passing the farm there is a stone stile which you cross and follow a lane for a short distance before crossing a ladder stile to follow the waymarkers across two fields on the eastern flank of Greeba.

There are superb views to the left over

Douglas as you head for the saddle between Greeba and Cronk ny Moghlane or Mucaillyn (hill of the sows) and the signpost on the skyline. After the next stile there is a diversion around the edge of the field before reaching the narrow road leading to Cronk Brec (hill of many colours. Literally piebald). You must now make a left and right to follow a rough stone track down to Ballaharry. Just before you reach the cottages look to the right and the sign pointing to an ancient monument. This is the site of the remains of Keeil Vreshey (the church of St. Bridget) and is an example of early Celtic Christianity - there were many such sites on the Island.

At Ballaharry the track joins a surfaced road which will take you into Crosby village at the crossroads with the main Douglas to Peel highway. Here you can finish the walk and return to Douglas by public transport or if you are really energetic you can carry on with the southern section of the walk to Castletown.

The southern section of the Millennium Way is totally different in character and the old 'regiam viam' would have passed to our left to cross between the Mount and Slieau Chiarn (the Lord's mountain). It has been incorporated into the present road network and in order to keep the walk more attractive the Way takes a slightly different but parallel route.

If you are just starting or if you have stopped at the local pub for lunch then it is a tough start. Make your way down Station Road - you will see where it gets its name as you pass the small crossing keepers house where the railway crossed the road. Then it is a stiff climb up School Hill passing the old school which was built in 1874. It's bleak location may seem a little strange when you look around and see where the centre of population is now. When it was built however the school was in the centre of the parish serving numerous remote farmsteads as well as the village.

Ballasalla

The same factors applied to the old parish church which you will pass at the top of the hill. The church is dedicated to St.Runius and dates from the 12th century although there is a record of an earlier keeil on the site, the remains of which can be seen, dating from the 7th century.

Continue along the road under the avenue of trees towards the Garth crossroads. Look out for the ancient monument sign on the right as you start to climb the next hill. It directs you to the site of St. Patrick's Chair which is a small group of stones where tradition has it that this is the spot where he first preached to the nation introducing Christianity to the Kingdom of Mann.

Carry straight on over the crossroads passing Ballanicholas and drop down the hill to Campbells Bridge marking the boundary between the parishes of Marown and Malew. Stop at the bridge which spans the Santon river to read the interesting plaque on the bridge and if you look over the bridge you may just be able to make out the remains of some mine workings.

Continue on past Shenvalley (old farm) and in the distance you will be able to see the tower of the church at St. Marks. The church is a good landmark and you will need to turn left and then right at St. Marks and around the old schoolhouse. The church , school and adjoining houses were built in the 18th. Century at the instigation of Bishop Hildesley as a chapel of ease to Malew parish church.

You need to be careful here and look for the waymarker beside the old parsonage. The path follows the lane beside the parsonage to the Awin Ruy (red river) which is crossed on an old stone slab. The path meanders through the fields of Upper and Lower Ballagarey (farm of the river thicket) crossing hedges through kissing gates eventually arriving at a surfaced road.

Cross the road and follow the waymarkers through two fields before entering Ballamodha Mooar farm yard and following the farm road through Ballamodha Beg to its junction with the Ballamodha Road (Ballamodha meaning farm of the dog, Mooar meaning big, and Beg little).

Turn left and walk along the road for approximately a mile taking care as there is no footpath. The Ballamodha straight was used in the past for motor car hill climbs and reliability trials when the motor car was in its infancy.

Continue to the bottom of Silverburn hill and at the Atholl Bridge turn left into Silverdale and walk on a riverbank path alongside the river. Approaching Silverdale you will walk into a children's playground, boating lake and café. The boating lake gives the clue to the function of the old building adjoining the café which was the Creg Mill one of two built by the Monks of Rushen Abbey. The boating lake was the dam providing the power for the mill wheel. The little water wheel which powers the children's roundabout is worth more than a passing glance as it came from the Foxdale Mines when they closed.

Continuing downstream we pass the site of more industry from the past where Ballasalla Ochre and Umber Works was located and is now converted into a private residence. The company was a substantial one and had warehousing in Castletown from where their shipments were made. The north quay still carries the name Umber Quay a reminder of the past activity.

Leaving the wooded glen you emerge through a gate at Monk's Bridge which is probably the oldest bridge in the Island dating from the late 13th early 14th century and built by the Monks of Rushen Abbey.

Approaching the site of the Abbey look to the left on the opposite side of the river and you will see the Abbey Mill which is now converted to private apartments. It was a substantial mill and had an internal water wheel and gives an indication of the importance of the Abbey. The whole area of the Abbey has now been acquired by Manx National Heritage and archeological research is now in progress to unfold the history of the site before it is incorporated into the Story of Mann.

Follow the boundary wall of the Abbey to the right and walk around the perimeter - you may be able to catch the odd glimpse of some of the remains through a gate on the way. Cross the road and almost opposite the waymarkers will direct you down a narrow lane and then left to the river again. The Way follows the river into Castletown on a pleasant walk through river meadows. You will cross the river on a wooden bridge continuing on the other side of the river nearer to the steam railway. Look for the weir that took water from the river for the Golden Meadow Mill which you will be able to see from the path as we pass Poulsom Park. The railway station is across the park and you can return to Douglas from there or continue into Castletown and finish your walk at the Castle.

Eventful Isle of Man

The Isle of Man runs a year-round programme of special events for visitors. The Island, like every Celtic nation, has proved a tradition of promoting its arts and culture. Perhaps most famously the Island is known for two, three and four-wheeled events, which attract visitors from all over Europe to the road-racing capital of the world. Listed below are some of the main attractions held annually. Readers are recommended to contact the Tourist Information Centre at Douglas for further information. The annual Tourist Board guide also catalogues information on the events of the year and the Tourist Information Centre also produces a monthly Events list.

The main Calendar of Events on the Island are as follows:

March

Isle of Man Open Darts Championships

April

Student Festival of Sport

May

Isle of Man Food and Drink Festival
Youth 2 Day Motorcycle Trial
International Whitsun Hockey Festival
Pre TT Classic Motorcycle races
TT Festival Fortnight
Round the Island Yacht Race

June

TT Festival Fortnight (May/June)
Ramsey Sprint
Steam Packet Road Races (Motorcycles)
Crown Green Bowling Festival
International Cycle Week
Isle of Man Open Sheep Dog Trials

July

The Historic Laxey Fair
Tynwald Day (Manx National Day)
Southern 100 Road Races (Motorcycles)
Yn Chruinnaght Inter Celtic Festival
Shakespeare in Peel Castle
Southern District Agricultural Show

August

Peel Carnival
Isle of Man Marathon and Half Marathon
Isle of Man Road Running Grand Prix
Manx Grand Prix Fortnight (Aug/Sept)
International Jazz Festival
Mannin Angling Week
Ramsey Angling Week
Royal Manx Agricultural Show
Ramsey Lifeboat Day

September

Manx Classic Weekend Motorcycle Trial
Manannan Opera Festival, Port Erin
International Car Rally
Crown Green Bowling Festival
Manx Last Night at the Proms
Manx Classic Car Races

November

Manannan International Winter Festival

Tynwald Day

Yn Chruinnaght

Tynwald Day

Royal Manx Agricultural Show

Shakespeare at Peel Castle

Index